THE EVOLVING EDUCATIONAL

MISSION OF THE LIBRARY

Betsy Baker
Mary Ellen Litzinger
Editors

Randall Hensley
Beth Sandore
Associate Editors

Bibliographic Instruction Section
Association of College and Research Libraries
A Division of the American Library Association
1992

D1445004

Published by the Association of College and Research Libraries
A Division of the American Library Association
50 East Huron Street
Chicago, IL 60611-2795

ASSOCIATION OF
COLLEGE
& RESEARCH
LIBRARIES
A DIVISION OF THE
AMERICAN LIBRARY ASSOCIATION

ISBN: 0-8389-7584-4

This publication is printed on recycled, acid-free paper.

Printed in the United State of America.

CONTRIBUTORS

Betsy Baker

Bill Coons

Elizabeth Frick

Martha Hale

Randall Hensley

Donald Kenney

Mary Ellen Litzinger

William Miller

Maureen Pastine

Hannelore Rader

Beth Sandore

James Shedlock

Linda Wilson

Lizabeth A. Wilson

TABLE OF CONTENTS

THE FUTURE OF BIBLIOGRAPHIC INSTRUCTION AND INFORMATION LITERACY FOR THE ACADEMIC LIBRARIAN

PREFACE

The ALA Conference in San Francisco in 1981 was an important one for bibliographic instruction. It was especially memorable for me. As a relative newcomer to association activities, the experience was not only interesting, but also challenging. I remember squirming in an uncomfortable chair, in a room too small for the hundreds of librarians crammed into it, to hear speakers at the Bibliographic Instruction Section program. I was sitting with two friends and former colleagues: Betsy Baker, who was also just beginning to find her feet in organizational activities, and Maureen Pastine, who was much more knowledgeable and experienced. When Brian Nielsen presented his paper *"Teacher or Intermediary: Alternative Professional Models in the Information Age,"* I finally realized why it had stimulated such conversation and controversy over the preceding few days. And I realized that a significant and formative event had occurred.

Only days before, the Bibliographic Instruction Section had sponsored a preconference. Most of us attended for the workshops and networking opportunities. But in conjunction with the occasion, seven leaders in the growing discipline had been brought together to discuss the issues and trends affecting bibliographic instruction. Nielsen's paper, which he had shared with the six other participants at the outset, had surely precipitated much discussion during that first "Think Tank," just as Fran Hopkins' paper must have offered a unique platform for viewing the discipline. The recommendations that derived from that Think Tank is but a skeletal reflection of the depth and breadth of thought and analysis these librarians had brought to bear in their conferences over those few days. And I remember thinking, while Nielsen was presenting his paper at the program, how stimulating those discussions must have been, rich in ideas and perspective.

Over the next six years, many of us benefitted from the insights of that Think Tank. But that half decade moved quickly. In 1981, the number of academic libraries with online catalogs was a minority. By 1986, technology was radically reshaping our services and redefining our professional roles as we rapidly moved into end-user searching, CD-ROM, and integrated systems. The character of our campuses was changing. And the level of our instructional thinking was evolving: critical thinking, problem solving, information literacy, information management education.

At the Midwinter Meeting of ALA in San Antonio in 1987, the Advisory Committee of the Bibliographic Instruction Section considered a proposal by Joe Boisse. The next Annual Conference was again slated for San Francisco; the location and timing was ripe for another Think Tank. Unfortunately, although all of us on the Advisory Committee concurred that the opportunity was fortuitous and the need imminent, six months just did not allow for adequate preparation, and funding was an insuperable problem. Betsy Baker, by then Chair of the Section, asked Joe Boisse and Mary Ellen Litzinger to flesh out a more complete planning document exploring the objectives and required resources.

In 1988, the second Think Tank then began to take shape. I was incoming Chair of the Bibliographic Instruction Section and Joe Boisse was the new President of ACRL. One of Joe's first accomplishments was the creation of the ACRL

Preface

Special Grants program to support innovative projects within the Division. Among my first priorities was to write a proposal to ACRL for funding of a second bibliographic instruction Think Tank to take place prior to the 1989 ALA Annual Conference in Dallas. ACRL allocated $2000 from its Special Grants funds to support the project. I immediately appointed a Think Tank Steering Committee with the charge of planning and implementing the Think Tank. Chaired by Betsy Baker, whose term in office had been completed, the committee included Melanie Dodson, Beth Sandore, Deborah Campana, and Randall Hensley. Because of Mary Ellen Litzinger's role in the early Think Tank proposals, Betsy Baker invited her to serve with her as co-chair of the Steering Committee. The Committee worked closely with the ACRL offices in Chicago for a year, and the expertise and support of JoAn Segal and Cathleen Bourdon were indispensable in this effort.

It is important to clarify that, although funded by ACRL and established by the Bibliographic Instruction Section, the Think Tank was much more than a Section project. The intent was to bring together individuals with innovative ideas and unique perspectives for two days of creative brainstorming on the subject of bibliographic instruction. Although the Steering Committee reported to the Bibliographic Instruction Section's Executive Committee, it was directed to function quite independently. It was important that the Think Tank transcend the views and purposes of current Section practices and agendas. It is to be expected under such circumstances that the ideas and recommendations that resulted would spark controversy, just as had the first Think Tank in San Francisco. However, the conscientiousness, dedication and responsibility with which the Steering Committee brought the Think Tank to fruition is evident in Betsy Baker's introductory chapter to this mono-graph, and their dedication to the project has benefitted us all.

The outcomes of the Think Tank were discussed in open forums during the Dallas Annual Conference and summaries have been published elsewhere. However, those sources cannot offer the full depth and breadth of thought that converged during the Think Tank. Although each Think Tank participant prepared an initial paper or a foundation for the discussions that occurred in San Francisco, this volume is much more than a seminar proceedings. Rather than serving as a set of Think Tank proceedings, this monograph offers us the considered thought and ideas of Think Tank participants as they evolved during the discussions and in the following months. In this way, we all have an opportunity to share in the creative forces that shape our discipline and push bibliographic instruction toward the future. Special thanks are due to Betsy Baker and Mary Ellen Litzinger for their editorial efforts, to Scott McDonald, and Marilee Birchfield, for their assistance to the editors, special thanks to Kathy Ryan and Marsha Holden all of Northwestern University Library and especially to Vera Marie Taylor and Melissa Jacobi also of Northwestern University Library, without whom the final preparation of the volume would have been impossible.

David N. King
January 1992

INTRODUCTION

At the 1981 ACRL/Bibliographic Instruction Section Preconference on Library Instruction, a panel of librarians was formed to discuss and debate issues related to bibliographic instruction. This symposium, which became known as the "BIS Think Tank," was noteworthy because it focused on universal intellectual, philosophical, and social issues rather than the methodological and practical concerns of implementing a bibliographic instruction program. Many of the ideas discussed in this meeting were explored under the rubric of preparing the "second generation" of instruction librarians to embrace future concerns. The major output of this effort--a collection of papers written by the Think Tank participants--was published in 1987 (Mellon, 1987).

In the ensuing decade, technological, social, and educational developments significantly altered the environment in which "second generation" librarians developed their instructional programs. A scant two years earlier, in November, 1979, the first White House Conference on Libraries and Information Service had been held, which drew public attention to Americans' increased need for "more and better access to knowledge" (Galvin, 1981). This energy prompted the creation of numerous technology-related organizational outlets within the American Library Association. In this work, a common thread of discussion is the concern about handling "access to excess."

Automation, which was barely recognized in 1981 as a factor in instructional programs, and only then in conjunction with online catalogs, permanently changed the nature of user interaction with libraries--on all levels. By the end of the decade, computer technology was a major factor in determining how library users obtained information.

American society, including such commonplace activities as using banks and telephones, has undergone a phenomenal shift in emphasis from communication using the written word to communication via images. McLuhan's earlier prediction that "the medium is the message" has come to fruition within many classes of society--the current "MTV generation" of students 18-22 years old, or older adults whose favorite pastimes revolve around watching TV, either for leisure entertainment or to keep informed by the daily news. As early as 1970, Dervin and Greenberg (1972) had determined that even 95% of poor households in the U.S. owned one television, with 40% owning two or more. Visual technology and communication are now integral to all aspects of our daily lives.

Concurrent with the electronic movement, the population of library users themselves has changed. The traditional college student of 18-22 years of age is joined by increasing numbers of returning adults, minorities, extended degree, international, and commuting students. The call for curriculum reform, exemplified by such reports as *A Nation at Risk*, (U.S. National Commission on Excellence in Education, 1983), emphasizes the need for developing critical thinking skills that would enable a diverse population of students to evaluate the enormous amount of data produced by the information explosion.

A Nation of Readers at Risk

The combined events of the 80's produced a perspective of value on information, and convenience of access to information, which now stands foremost in the minds of users. In the

Introduction

field of library and information science, a positive outlook toward the mission of literacy has been adopted. Juxtaposed with the concerns of the authors of *A Nation at Risk* is the popular ALA slogan, "a nation of readers," created with the intention of promoting readership. However, the real concern of BI librarians about users' lack of critical information seeking and evaluation skills might be summed up in the phrase "A nation of readers at risk." Across U.S. campuses, the risk of losing the opportunity to promote student readership and critical thinking skills increases steadily as librarians fail to evaluate and change current print-based instruction methods in libraries.

By the end of the 1980's, it was clear that the time was ripe for examining a new set of issues, using the successful format of the first Think Tank. The Association of College and Research Libraries recognized this fact and agreed to sponsor a second Think Tank, which was held in Dallas, Texas immediately preceding the 1989 annual meeting of the American Library Association. "Think Tank II" was used as a dynamic mechanism for exploring future directions both in the discipline of library user education and for the Bibliographic Instruction Section of ACRL. Ten participants were chosen through nomination:

William Coons (Cornell University)
Elizabeth Frick (Dalhousie University)
Martha Hale (Emporia State University)
Allison Level (Emporia State University)
William Miller (Florida Atlantic University)
Maureen Pastine (Southern Methodist University)
Hannelore Rader (Cleveland State University)

James Shedlock (Northwestern University)
Lizabeth Wilson (University of Illinois)
Linda Wilson (Virginia Tech. University)

Discussion centered on these issues:

1) Who are our primary user groups and how have they changed during the past decade?
2) How does the curricular reform movement affect the content of bibliographic instruction programs?
3) Is "information literacy" an appropriate phrase to characterize BI librarians' instructional programs for the upcoming decade?
4) How can professional education programs in library and information science respond to these changes?

These particular issues had been identified within numerous BI Circles as major influences from changes in the focus of higher education in the United States.

The Think Tank Steering Committee, co-chaired by Betsy Baker, Northwestern University, and Mary Ellen Litzinger, Penn State University, planned and coordinated the symposium. Members of the committee included Deborah Campana (Northwestern University), Melanie Dodson (New York University), Randall Hensley (University of Washington), and Beth Sandore (University of Illinois).

Introduction

Think Tank II Outcomes

The Think Tank promoted the expression of a healthy diversity of opinions. Each of the Think Tank participants prepared a position paper and led a portion of the retreat focusing on one of the above topics. As the position papers were presented and discussed, the ideas which emerged from the group formed a series of concentric circles. The four discussion issues suggested necessary change or transition, particularly for BI, but more broadly affecting reference and public service, library missions and goals, and the educational focus of the library information science profession. While participants viewed each subject from different vantage points, they agreed emphatically on three recommendations:

> 1) *Link BI with information literacy*: regardless of semantic differences, the group emphasized that it is critical for BI librarians to address broader instructional issues than those contained within the walls of the library, and to make their presence visible on campus, and throughout the user community;
> 2) *Strengthen the Library education mission*: the profession must seek new and creative ways to foster the development of professionals who can ultimately carry the goals of instruction forward;
> 3) *Reward leadership* within the profession, regardless of how controversial, especially when it contributes to valuable innovation.

Think Tank participants suggested numerous objectives which could be adopted to help meet these goals (see Appendix A, "Think Tank Summary Document.")

After the Think Tank, pairs of participants who had collaborated on Think Tank position papers moved forward to further synthesize their ideas and the feedback which was received during the course of the Think Tank and resultant discussions both within and beyond BIS. The authors were charged with the responsibility of placing their own ideas within the context of the evolving educational role of the library vis a vis the changing agenda reflected in higher education. The resulting papers represent not one cohesive perspective, but rather several equally valid views on key educational issues which now face the library profession. Some of the ideas presented are found in the mainstream of the profession. Others suggest that BI librarians seek a new interpretation of their role and its relationship to information use, evaluation, and management, and, perhaps most importantly, the concept of service provision. While these suggestions will likely create dissonance within BI, they are intended to act as catalysts to invoke discussion and innovation within the profession.

In the first chapter, Donald Kenney, a participant in the 1981 Think Tank, draws parallels between the issues discussed at the two retreats. Kenney observes that both the impact of technology and the shift in instructional perspective from a local to global orientation have contributed to the greatest changes and accomplishments within BI.

Bonnie Frick, in her chapter "The Think Tank Papers: Are We in the Ballpark?" views the challenges facing instruction librarians as part of an ever-changing continuum, ministering to both traditional and emerging user information needs. She

Introduction

notes that librarians "are adapting not just to the new technologies but also to the revised ways of thinking about the world...while at the same time watching the growth of traditional issues: good service and universal access."

Maureen Pastine and Linda Wilson explore the impact of curricular reform on the mission of academic libraries, arguing that an increased emphasis on independent learning and continuing education focuses attention on the need for developing lifelong information access skills. Librarians are in a unique position to advocate resource-based learning across all disciplines, but such advocacy requires a restructuring of the traditional "reactive" role model to become initiators, designers and facilitators of curricular change.

Lizabeth Wilson explores the impact of changing user populations in the chapter "Changing Users: Bibliographic Instruction for Whom?" Wilson explores the library's traditional definitions of library user groups and predicts how they will change during the next decade. In particular, she highlights the role of changing undergraduate populations, the boost in minority enrollments, and changes in international student enrollments, in effecting this change. Wilson also discusses the effects of technological change on student populations within the academic library setting and makes instructional recommendations which will accommodate their diverse and evolving information needs.

James Shedlock explores the impact of the changing medical library user on the development of bibliographic instruction, coining the phrase "information management education" as a synonym for the concept of bibliographic instruction. Shedlock notes that librarians in the health sciences fields are responsive to what they perceive are the changing information needs of their users, hence the development of programs that feature technology as a primary teaching tool.

Although Shedlock maintains that "information management" and "bibliographic instruction" are synonymous terms, Bill Coons and Hannelore Rader argue in their chapter that information literacy programs will more effectively address the information gathering and managing needs of today's library users than current bibliographic instruction programs. They assert that information literacy differs, both in concept and method, from traditional BI; whereas bibliographic instruction represents a "situation-specific" approach to user education, information literacy "contributes to life-long learning by educating individuals to effectively utilize and evaluate information." Like Pastine and Wilson, they call for librarians to address instructional issues on a campus-wide scale.

Inherent in any discussion involving professional change is the concern about corresponding changes in the professional curriculum. Martha Hale notes a shift in the paradigm of the library and information science discipline which responds to the influence of technology and the changing image of the profession. Hale proposes that library education shift its focus from a narrow "biblio" or book-centered focus to an "information transfer" focus:

> If the focus in curricula is broadened to INFORMATION (recorded, visual, oral, and graphic) TRANSFER (including creation, diffusion, and utilization), the library profession has a great chance that the first learned behaviors of graduates will be broad rather than narrow.

xx

Introduction

In the final chapter, William Miller comments on the fact that BI has become a mainstream library activity, evidenced by the widespread acceptance and support of BI as a permanent program within reference departments, and as a primary component in library goal and mission statements. However, Miller notes that, since the sweeping acceptance of instructional programs in libraries, the profession has moved to a point where traditional BI programs are not sufficient "to carry the library profession into the electronic age." Miller also eloquently articulates a challenge to the library's position in an academic community which is resource-poor and increasingly critical of our professional standing:

> Regardless of how willing the profession is to move from bibliographic instruction to information literacy, there remains open the question of whether society will grant librarians the right to play this teaching role.... This country has no tradition of viewing libraries, even academic libraries, as more than warehouses that offer triage service. So the road ahead will be difficult at best.

However, Miller believes that librarians are the most likely candidates to fill this role for several reasons, including the profession's high credibility, strong base of teaching talent, and traditionally strong social role for helping people with information needs.

The development of any movement requires much forethought and considerable philosophical iteration before action and progress can be observed. The manuscripts in this collection, which articulate the issues now influencing the educational role of academic libraries, represent the beginning of this iteration. The responsibility for continuing this dialog rests with all professionals who administer and participate in bibliographic instruction programs. Their combined efforts will shape the agenda that greets the "third generation" of bibliographic instruction librarians.

As with any movement, those involved in BI identify with one or more generation in its development. Those who helped gain the first toehold for BI in reference services in the 1970's recall the first-generation emphasis on BI as library orientation. In the 1980's, the second generation of BI enabled the development of ideas and methods, and saw the positioning of BI as an integral component of reference services. The third and nascent generation of BI will see the inevitable shift in focus from solely print-oriented library services toward information provision in numerous formats, using multi-media, for diverse user groups. The opportunity to build beyond the firmly established foundation of the second generation to establish the third generation is an exciting challenge which we believe this book has helped to launch.

Betsy Baker
Mary Ellen Litzinger
Beth Sandore
Randall Hensley

Introduction

References

Dervin, Brenda and Bradley S. Greenberg. "The communication environment of the urban poor." In *Current perspectives in mass communications research*. F. G. Kline and P. J. Tichenor (eds.) Beverly Hills: Sage, 1972, pp. 195-233.

Mellon, Constance A. (ed.) *Bibliographic Instruction: the Second Generation*. Littleton, CO: Libraries Unlimited, 1987.

United States. National Commission on Excellence in Education. "A nation at risk: the imperative for education reform: a report to the Nation and the Secretary of Education, United States Department of Education, by the National Commission on Excellence in Education. Washington, D.C.: Superintendent of Documents, U.S. Government Printing Office. April, 1983.

BRIDGING THE GAP BETWEEN THE THINK TANKS

Donald Kenney

Significant events in history tend to be recalled in terms of milestones. While there have been numerous milestones in the evolution of library instruction, two important events stand out for the instructional movement. Having been a participant in the 1981 Think Tank on Bibliographic Instruction in San Francisco, I see that event as an important milestone. A similar event occurred in Dallas, Texas in June 1989 when the Association of College and Research Libraries' (ACRL) Bibliographic Instruction Section (BIS) sponsored a second Think Tank. Both of these events addressed long-standing issues and problems such as changing technologies, library users and their needs, and the role of academic libraries and librarians in higher education. To some extent, the real value of the think tank process was to encourage the profession to think more globally in terms of information.

Since Think Tank I, numerous changes have occurred in academic libraries, changes that have required librarians to respond in nontraditional ways. Changing technologies have played a tremendous role in bibliographic instruction. The pace at which new technologies have influenced library instruction has placed technology at the forefront of discussions at conferences, meetings, and workshops. Users have always been at the center of concern for instructional librarians, and identifying our users and their bibliographic instruction needs is of great concern to the profession. The role of the academic library and librarians in higher education is a central issue related to bibliographic instruction. These themes played an important role in the deliberations of Think Tanks I and II.

Looking Back: Think Tank I

The first Think Tank was held as part of the 1981 ACRL/BIS Preconference on Library Instruction in San Francisco. Six librarians were selected to take part from nominations solicited through notices in the professional literature. Selection criteria primarily focused on participants' practical experience in planning and implementing a bibliographic instruction program as well as their contributions to conferences, meeting presentations, and publications. The librarians selected were Frances Hopkins, Head of Reference, Temple University; Donald Kenney, Head of General Reference, Virginia Tech; Brian Nielsen, Head of Reference, Northwestern University; Anne Roberts, Coordinator of Library Instruction, SUNY-Albany; Carla Stoffle, Assistant Chancellor for Educational Services, University of Wisconsin-Parkside; and Paula Walker, Library Instruction Coordinator, University of Washington. Joanne Euster, Director of the Library, San Francisco State University, was selected to lead this group.

Discussions focused on the broad intellectual, philosophical, and social issues surrounding library instruction rather than daily administrative and methodological issues. As described in "Think Tank Recommendations for Bibliographic Instruction" printed in *College and Research Libraries News* 42 (December 1981), the group's discussion focused on three important themes: 1) "building bridges" throughout the library profession, but more importantly, to the academic community and to library schools; 2) encouraging research and publication; 3) and developing an underlying pedagogy of bibliographic instruction.

Think Tank participants hoped that their discussion of these ideas would form the basis for subsequent consideration by the "second generation" of bibliographic instruction librarians.

The importance of Think Tank I is evident both from the response to its recommendations and the resulting literature. The report was presented in draft form at the final session of the Preconference in San Francisco. Judy Reynolds, one of the organizers of the Preconference stated in a letter to Carla Stoffle that this report was received with "interest, enthusiasm, and even a little controversy." The assertions that bibliographic instruction was not a secondary function of a reference librarian or reference unit, and that the activities performed at a reference or informational service point were mop-up activities for instruction proved to be highly controversial. As a follow up to the report, the *Journal of Academic Librarianship* published a symposium called "Reactions to the Think Tank Recommendations" (March 1983). In the major output of Think Tank I, *Bibliographic Instruction: The Second Generation*, edited by Constance A. Mellon (1987), Carla Stoffle and Cheryl Bernero challenged the "second generation" to "address the issue of definitions and labels for the instructional activity." This challenge paved the way for the second Think Tank.

The Ties That Bind: Think Tank I and II

When Think Tank I met in San Francisco in 1981, librarians had just begun to recognize the impact of computer technology. Most academic libraries were dealing with the problems of implementing an online catalog system. Aside from the many technical problems this transition presented to the profession, librarians confronted profound questions and problems in making these new systems available to users. The issues of user access to online systems figured prominently in the discussion on technology. Think Tank II participants faced a more dramatic technological development: the impact of CD-ROMs and end-user searching on information access.

Both generations of librarians feel strongly that biblio-graphic instruction should be integrated into the university curriculum. This integration provides librarians with a legitima-cy equal to that of the teaching faculty. Indeed, students' reception and perception of bibliographic instruction often depends on its equivalent footing with individual course requirements in the curriculum.

No discussion of bibliographic instruction can possibly occur without considering users--the people librarians see as the beneficiaries of instruction. University and college populations have indeed changed over the years between the two Think Tanks. The identity of a library's users will continue to influence and provide direction for its instruction. To some extent, the changing college and university populations have stimulated library instruction. The influx of the nontraditional student--older adults returning for a university education and advanced degrees--helped to start the instructional movement. Librarians perceived a need to help these students who were not tied to traditional scholarly fields. Think Tank II continued to explore the boundaries of bibliographic instruction and the changing user population in today's university setting.

Changing technology has had a sweeping impact on academic libraries. The transition from card catalogs to computerized online systems forced academic librarians to design new job roles and serve a more diverse clientele. With the advent of networking capabilities and easy access to national bibliographic databases, librarians are confronted with teaching users who may never enter the doors of the library. Remote access will continue to grow as full text databases are made available to users. The challenge for bibliographic instruction will be to develop teaching strategies to meet the needs of these users.

In the last decade, the growth of information was a widely recognized issue. Computer technologies have accelerated the distribution of information. Today's instructional librarian not only has to consider what access tools to teach, but also how to sift through the volume of information available in printed and electronic sources.

Think Tank II and The Future Agenda

Participants in Think Tank II raised important questions and issues for the future. Those selected by nomination were Bill Coons, Information Literacy Librarian, Mann Library, Cornell University; Elizabeth Frick, Associate Professor, Dalhousie University; Martha Hale, Dean of the School of Library and Information Management, Emporia State University; Allison Level, graduate student of Emporia State University; William Miller, Director of Libraries, Florida Atlantic University; Maureen Pastine, Director of the Library, Southern Methodist University; Hannelore Rader, Director of University Library, Cleveland State; James Shedlock, Director of Galter Health Sciences Medical Library, Northwestern University; Linda Wilson, Coordinator of Bibliographic Instruction, Virginia Tech; and Lizabeth Wilson, Head of the Undergraduate Library, University of Illinois at Urbana-Champaign.

One of the distinct differences between Think Tank I and Think Tank II was the approach each group developed in addressing the issues. Think Tank I participants met for two days of discussing, debating, pondering, and synthesizing. They came from different work environments and brought different experiences with bibliographic instruction programs to their discussions. Bibliographic instruction was still fighting its way into the classrooms and curriculum of colleges and universities around the country. While ACRL's Bibliographic Instruction Section had more members than any other section, the level of confidence in the discipline was uncertain.

Think Tank II was conducted under very different circumstances. Instead of discussing a group of issues, participants were asked to prepare and present papers. This approach marks a turning point for the section. The ability to be introspective and question the future of the discipline attests to the strength and maturity of the Section and its members.

Shaping and Sharpening My Personal Focus

Think Tank I helped to shape my attitudes and raise my personal consciousness about the role of library instruction in the academic setting. Prior to this experience, I saw library instruction as a service to the academic community rather than as an integral part of the academic curriculum. Our discussions during the Think Tank sessions challenged my perception of the traditional role that I was accustomed to playing, and changed how I thought the role of bibliographic instruction should evolve.

I don't know that being a participant in the first Think Tank changed the way I taught. If anything, it sensitized me to the potential role that librarians could play in influencing curriculum development in the academic environment. But most importantly, I realized that librarians did indeed have a role in influencing and developing the curriculum along with the faculty. A sense of reassurance that other librarians shared this viewpoint was somehow comforting to me.

This "confidence building" spilled over into my daily activities in dealing with a library administration that was not always supportive of bibliographic instruction functions. I headed a department that was charged with providing most instructional activities. The administration minimally supported these efforts, always holding out hope that I would not request monies from the budget to do anything instructionally oriented. Shortly after my attendance at the Think Tank, my library introduced its online catalog system. The administration, of course, turned to me to support and to develop the "instructional component." My department accepted the challenge and developed a comprehensive plan to introduce the university community to the new online system. However, the plan called for additional personnel, in particular a Project Manager, as well as funds for instructional materials, equipment to provide demonstrations throughout the campus, and the involvement of all librarians, in both public and technical services. In submitting the plan to the administration, I recalled the discussions we had in San Francisco, particularly the idea of placing instruction at the top of library priorities instead of at the end. Whether my participation in the Think Tank had anything to do with the eventual success in implementing this project is a matter of conjecture. I think it did.

Summary

Bibliographic instruction has moved well beyond its initial grassroots movement. It is no longer a movement in the realm of academic libraries--it is a force. With the advent of the computer age and the accessibility of more information via computers and telecommunications, no academic library can properly function or serve its faculty and student populations without providing instruction. The role bibliographic instruction must assume is to help users distinguish between information and knowledge. This skill will become crucial as more information is available to the user.

Think Tank I and II helped to advance the cause of library instruction. Both provided an opportunity for the profession to reflect upon its past and present, and to project its future; both events have been part of the maturing process while preparing us for the 1990s and the next century.

The papers in this collection are an introspective and reflective response to issues that affect the future of user education programs. The thoughts of these Think Tank participants will, like those of their predecessors, influence the agenda for the "third generation" of bibliographic instruction librarians.

THE THINK TANK PAPERS: ARE WE IN THE BALL PARK?

Elizabeth Frick

"Those who cannot remember the past are condemned to repeat it," said George Santayana (1932, 284) at the beginning of this century. It would be comforting to know that what has been termed the "second generation" of instruction librarians will not be thus doomed to repeat their history through ignorance. When an understanding of new trends in relationship to former ones is achieved, that understanding encourages action in the new circumstances with a wisdom born of the knowledge of the historical context in which librarians are operating.

Librarianship has always appeared as a conundrum to this writer: displaying both a need to cling to the old and to leap into the new. It was reassuring to read that another beloved institution suffers a similar schizophrenia. Will (1990, 293) states:

> baseball is both intensely traditional and interestingly progressive. By progressive I mean steadily improving. The traditional side is obvious in baseball's absorption with its past and its continuities.

Librarianship, too, must steadily improve while at the same time tending to its continuities.

Librarianship Then and Now

In the past century user instruction has moved through a number of phases. Indeed, the entire profession of librarianship/information service has moved through a number of phases. Both user instruction and librarianship itself began with an inward-turning absorption in the immediate task at hand, whether that task was getting an instruction course in place or building a collection. Later, librarians concentrated on the development of a theoretical grid of understanding through which order could be imposed on the perceived chaos, defining a logical order to the process of library research, or a hierarchical order to knowledge. Current thinking has moved to consideration of the need, not so much for a rigid order by which to comprehend external reality--whether students or recorded knowledge--as for an adaptation of library processes to the process of the external reality.

In the case of librarianship, this has meant evolving from a concentration on the collection of materials to an emphasis on organizing principles to a recognition of the primacy of the user. Michael Keresztesi (1982, 2) has said:

> Today, with the advent of the "information age,"
> we seem to have slipped into a new pattern. The
> library's function is being transformed from that
> of a public warehouse of cultural goods to one of
> a social dynamic institution of communication
> and knowledge dissemination.

One certainly can discern a move from an emphasis on collection and organization to a concept of service.

In bibliographic instruction, a similar pattern is evident. There has been a move from a concentration on how to initiate courses and what kinds of courses to initiate, through an attempt to impose an ordered logic on library research, to a concern for how to adapt teaching to the logic of the learner. Specifically, the issues originally debated were: How do librarians convince faculty of the importance of bibliographic instruction? In what terms should behavioral objectives be couched? Should overheads or computer assisted instruction (CAI) be used? Subsequently, authors such as Reichel and Ramey (1987), Kobelski and Reichel (1981), and Frick (1975) focused debates on search strategies and conceptual frameworks. Even while this focus was being developed, some writers were already expressing concerns with learning theory and educational psychology--with the nature of the user's learning patterns. Aluri (1981), Aluri and Reichel (1982), and Mellon and Sass (1981) all focused on the cognitive and affective aspects of users and on how these aspects should influence library programs.

Eadie (1989) states that subsequent phases do not eliminate the concerns of the earlier phases. In each phase new priorities take precedence in the call on professional energies. Perhaps these transitions reflect some logic of institutional development or perhaps of human development. Whatever their genesis, the transitions do seem to reflect a changing view of service.

Literacy Then and Now

In replacing the terms "user education" or "bibliographic instruction" with "information literacy," the significance of research in the field of literacy should not be ignored. Libraries are adopting the term "literacy" often without reflecting the complex ethical, social, and political approaches in the literacy field. While it is wise to heed Arp's (1990, 48) warning that "the term [literacy] connotes variant meanings to groups outside the field, and that there is a political agenda associated with the literacy movement," that should not mean that those ethical, social, and political implications can be ignored or underrated. The implications may be found to be rich ones for very traditional aims--providing the bridge being sought between continuities and the new environment.

The term literacy no longer means, for instance, that people in less developed countries should be able to read about Dick and Jane, Spot and Puff. It means that people everywhere should be able to express themselves and their culture with a mode of expression and in a written language that is closest to them. In his lucid way, Paulo Freire (1970, 10) wrote about the books he saw being used in adult literacy campaigns in Latin America in the early 1970s.

> Their authors do not recognize in the poor classes the ability to know and even create the texts which would express their own thought-language at the level of their perception of the world. The authors repeat with the texts what they do with the words, i.e., they introduce them into the learners' consciousness as if it were empty space...the "digestive" concept of knowledge.

And in a later book, Freire (1985, 89) states:

> From a methodological or sociological point of view, primers developed mechanistically, like any other texts, cannot escape a type of original sin however good they may be, since they are instruments for "depositing" the educator's words into

the learners. And since they limit the power of
expression and creativity, they are domesticating
instruments.

The empowerment of creativity and expression is based not in
the empowerer, but in the creator/expressor.
    There is a presumptuous tendency to use the word
literacy in the move to change from the term bibliographic
instruction to information literacy. In using the phrase information literacy, librarians are trading on the interest stirred by two
currently trendy words. Not only does this deliberately use the
term information to allude to the newer technologies, but it also
rides on a crest of current interest in basic literacy.

User Education As Information Literacy

Applying the kind of approach developed by literacy
experts such as Freire to bibliographic instruction, or information literacy, has at least three immediate implications. First,
that instruction or training for information literacy must be
experienced in the language and/or context of the learner.
Secondly, the methodologies used cannot be what Freire (1970)
describes as the "digestive" or, as he described in a later work
(1972), the "banking method of education." Thirdly, this
approach implies that instruction should be for the purpose of
empowerment of the learner.
    The instruction then is, firstly, based in the user's context
and terms. Instruction librarians have spoken often of the
teachable moment, of getting to the student at the time when
papers are initiated. Librarians have admonished one another
not to use terms such as "main entry" and "bibliography of
bibliographies" with the uninitiated. These terms reflect the
librarian's context rather than the user's context and terms.

Secondly, the research that precedes the instruction is, if it is to be effective, conducted in nontraditional terms of the user's context. It is interesting to hear Freire's (1972, 100) statement that "Men *are* because they *are in* a situation" mirrored in a newer and very different context--that of user research--by Brenda Dervin (1989, 230): "What is needed are categories that are communication-based--*situated and relevant to actors*". Evaluation, too, can very appropriately use qualitative methodologies with results that utilize the subject's own words.

Thirdly, the training is aimed not at fitting the learner into a precontrived niche, but at opening out for the learner the possibility of contriving his or her own niche to fit his or her own developing understandings of the world. If bibliographic instruction is significant, it is significant when it develops a user astute and flexible in information gathering. An intelligent approach to information involves the ability to apply learning obtained in one area to fresh problems, and to bring the skills of critical thinking to the process of information gathering. This approach is synonymous with the two highest levels of Bloom's (1974) taxonomy of objectives: synthesizing and evaluating. Such an approach to the process of information gathering looks at development as an open-ended process, and also from the perspective of the developer who defines his or her own context rather than from the predetermining perspective of the development teacher.

In an earlier presentation by this author (1990), the primary purpose of instruction was described as "the empowerment of people to better control, evaluate, and order their own information context." This latter aim of instruction, the empowerment of the user, is a difficult one to envision in a world where research, and the institutions of research, are seemingly set in ways that defy change or even the envisioning of change.

Empowerment of the user is, nevertheless, an aim redolent of tradition and worth contemplation in a new environment.

In this model of training for information literacy, the exercise of knowing the user becomes a critical one. And knowing goes beyond simple identification. It includes, as Lizabeth Wilson suggests in another chapter of this book, recognition of varying definitions or sight-lines of the user, and recognition of change in the backgrounds--educational, attitudinal, cultural--of the users themselves. For instance, there is a need to strengthen the understanding of many aspects of information gathering. Why do some people (and not others) use (or do not use) libraries? What factors influence their choice of materials? Why do they seek information? At what strategic points in the intellectual process do they seek information?

Miksa (1989) and other writers have alluded, either explicitly or implicitly, to this move to a user-defined environment. The outlines of this newer model of service remain undetermined. Writers still wrestle with the task of definition.

Further, if information is for the purpose of the empowerment of the user, concern must be given to how information is packaged so that it is most effective for the user. Packaging in this context can describe a number of daily situations. For the special librarian it may describe the survey and assessment of the literature that he or she completes for a researcher. For an online searcher it could be the explanation given of the dense acronyms used in a printout. A good reference librarian knows that the answer he or she gives is only the right answer when the user *perceives* its relevance and use. A systems designer is urged to supply a "user-friendly" (i.e., "most effective" for the user) system. Among other meanings "most effective" may mean "most relevant," "most readable," or "best organized." But always it means in the terms that are perceived relevant, readable, or organized *to the user*.

Conclusion

Some writers in areas of the profession closely related to information literacy are urging a new conceptualization; a new paradigm in the categories used to observe the user. Dervin's (1989) argument is that movement is needed toward a new paradigm that categorizes the user by quite novel categories-- ones that are significant to the user. Miksa's (1989) argument is that a new paradigm for library operations is needed--one that begins rather than ends with the user.

There is no argument that these are difficult issues. That they are irritating, the answers seemingly elusive, is evident. That they are powerful issues that will not go away must be faced.

Looked at from a relaxed stance, the more recent studies on bibliographic instruction have dealt with no issue that was not already inherent ten years ago. A more critical glance, however, reveals the (perhaps) uneasy awareness of a sharper edge to the issues raised, an increased sense of the significance of the choice of direction.

Library services such as bibliographic instruction will move into new areas that are in harmony with the areas society is exploring, e.g., advanced technology, new disciplines, fresh methodologies. At the same time, the older verities are tended, e.g., freedom of expression, the primacy of access.

The term "tended" brings two metaphors to mind. One is the metaphor of the shepherd tending his sheep. The shepherd is pictured as collecting, herding, accounting for, protecting his charges. Another, significantly different meta- phor is of the gardener tending a garden. In this metaphor the tending relates to cultivating, ensuring an environment conducive to growth, and benefitting from growth and change. The gardener is the image most appropriately allied to the concerns of professional librarians--tending the issues even while the issues are being redefined. According to Santayana (1932, 280), "Progress, far from consisting in change, depends on retentiveness." It is from this stance that the library profession's thinkers must help to move the profession steadily in consort with what is termed progress in society, while at the same time tending to the issues that have been continuing hallmarks of the profession. In some ways good service does not mean what it formerly meant. It is, nevertheless, still a root aim. Issues are changing yet the root is still there. Progress is complex.

It is in this ballpark that librarians are adapting not just to the new technologies but also to the revised ways of thinking about the world that are both the causes and the effects of those new technologies, while at the same time watching the growth of traditional issues: good service and universal access.

There is urgency to the game. While the process of redefining terms goes on, the margin for error has narrowed considerably.

References

Aluri, Rao. 1981. Application of learning theories to library-use instruction, *Libri* 31 (August): 140-152.

Aluri, Rao and Mary Reichel. 1982. Evaluation of student learning in library-use instruction programs based on cognitive learning theory. In *Proceedings: Second International Conference on Library User Education*, edited by Peter Fox. Loughborough: INFUSE.

Arp, Lori. 1990. Information literacy or bibliographic instruction: Semantics or philosophy? 30 *RQ* (Fall): 48.

Bloom, Benjamin S. et al. 1974. *The Taxonomy of Educational Objectives: Affective and Cognitive Domains*. New York: David McKay.

Dervin, Brenda. 1989. Users as research inventions: How research categories perpetuate inequities. *Journal of Communication*. 39 (Summer): 216-232.

Eadie, Tom. 1990. Immodest proposals: User instruction for students does not work. *Library Journal* 15 (October): 42-45.

Freire, Paulo. 1970. The adult literacy process as cultural action for freedom. In *Cultural Action for Freedom*. Cambridge, MA: Harvard Educational Review and the Center for the Study of Development and Social Change. Originally published in the *Harvard Educational Review* 40 (May 1970).

Freire, Paulo. 1972. *Pedagogy of the Oppressed*. Translated by Myra Bergaman Ramos. New York: Herder and Herder.

Freire, Paulo. 1985. *The Politics of Education*. South Hadley, MA: Bergin & Garvey.

Frick, Elizabeth. 1975. Information structure and bibliographic instruction. *The Journal of Academic Librarianship* 1 (September): 12-14.

Keresztesi, Michael. 1982. The science of bibliography: Theoretical implications for bibliographic instruction. *Theories of Bibliographic Education: Designs for Teaching.* eds. Cerise Oberman and Katina Strauch. New York: Bowker.

Kobleski, Pamea and Mary Reichel. 1975. Conceptual frameworks for bibliographic instruction. *The Journal of Academic Librarianship* 7 (May): 73-77.

Mellon, Constance and Edmund Sass. 1981. Perry and Piaget: Theoretical framework for effective college course development. *Educational Technology* 21 (May): 29-33.

Miksa, Francis. 1989. The future of reference II: A paradigm of academic library organization. *College and Research Libraries News* 40 (October): 780-790.

Reichel, Mary and Mary Ann Ramey, ed. 1987. *Conceptual Frameworks for Bibliographic Education: Theory into Practice.* Littleton, CO: Libraries Unlimited.

Santayana, George. 1932. *The Life of Reason Or the Phases of Human Progress*, 2nd ed., vol. 1. New York: Scribner's.

Will, George F. 1990. *Men at Work: The Craft of Baseball.* New York: Macmillan.

CHANGING USERS: BIBLIOGRAPHIC INSTRUCTION FOR WHOM?

Lizabeth A. Wilson

The adage "the more things change, the more they stay the same" does not apply to academic library users. By only looking around academic libraries, listening to exchanges at the reference desk, and observing in classrooms, it becomes apparent that users in college and university libraries have changed significantly over the past ten years.

The view from the reference desk is particularly enlightening as the following examples demonstrate. Take the patron you judge to be a professor, who turns out to be a new graduate student in finance who has come back to school in order to make a career change. In a somewhat hushed tone, the patron confides that the number of computers in use in the library is a little overwhelming.

Or how about the person who asks, "Where is the computer that lists all the books, magazine articles, statistics, definitions, and quotes needed for a term paper?" You explain that no such magic machine exists, but that you would be pleased to assist in finding material using a variety of computer and print databases.

You answer the reference desk phone. It's a somewhat harried caller, frustrated by not being able to dial into the library's catalog. The caller wonders if the library could send someone over to the office to help connect a newly purchased modem.

Observe the newly arrived international student milling around, avoiding the reference desk, but obviously in search of something. A patron approaches a fellow student and asks for assistance in finding books.

Consider the patron who can't believe that interlibrary loan could take up to three weeks. Certainly, the user asks, the article could be faxed or optically scanned and sent to an electronic mail address.

Librarians are increasingly seeing panicked students in their bibliographic instruction classes. It's not that they can't find the information they need, but that there is too much information. How do they begin to decide which source is better than the next? Where do they go from here?

You're teaching a class in research skills and an African-American student asks why there isn't anything under "Blacks in Accounting" in the catalog. The student asks, "Doesn't the library have any material on minorities in the professions?" You begin, once again, your often repeated explanation of the historical development of subject headings.

Take a walk around the library, and the view continues to reflect the changing users in academic libraries. The once popular individual carrels are easily had; the competition is for group study tables, conference rooms, and informal gathering space. In the CD-ROM site, pairs and trios of students hover around a terminal. Together they search the databases, suggest alternative strategies, and teach one another the ins and outs of the technology.

Technology has transformed the library, but a tour around the place points up how it has also changed users and their search behaviors. The computer print-outs emanating from the online catalogs, the CD-ROM terminals, and the microcomputer site produce an ever present din. It seems as if every other student wears a walkman as they read, research, converse, and write. An occasional student is taking notes using a lap-top computer. Students in the microcomputer laboratory are sending their term papers to their instructors via the campus network. They are downloading citations from the online catalog and the CD-ROM databases for instant bibliographies. Every video viewing station is booked as students watch a documentary for class, professors preview possible media material for incorporation into their courses, and second language learners of English watch contemporary films to catch slang in action. Just think, ten years ago, this library had three 300-baud ASCII terminals for searching the automated circulation system. Today the library supports thirty-five microcomputers in an open-access site linked to the campus network, fourteen CD-ROM workstations, eighteen online catalog terminals, ten office microcomputers, two interactive video workstations, four writing instruction terminals, a career diagnostic microcomputer, three PLATO terminals, three instructional development microcomputers, and a search strategy expert system terminal. To grow from three to ninety-one computer terminals in ten years is a thirty-fold increase in the hardware base. While the numbers are indeed staggering, the implications for users are even more significant.

The view from the reference desk, in the classroom, and around the library provides engaging anecdotal pictures of the changes taking place in libraries and with the users. But who are the users? How have the users changed in the last ten years? Who will the users be ten years from now as the century mark is reached? And what does all of this mean for bibliographic instruction? This paper will attempt to address these four questions and in doing so answer the ultimate question: "Bibliographic Instruction for Whom?"

Who Are the Library's Users?

When determining who the users are, librarians must first consider whose definition of "user" is being used. Consciously or not, academic librarians operate with three, not necessarily exclusive, but sometimes conflicting definitions of user: 1) the profession's definition; 2) the institution's definition; and 3) the self-selection definition.

The profession's definition, as learned in library school, is that everyone is a user or a potential user of libraries. Librarians are committed to providing free and equal access to information for the citizenry while recognizing the value of broad dissemination and critical use of information to ensure an informed society; this is a basic tenet of a democracy. The professional definition speaks in almost missionary terms of the goal of reaching the served as well as the unserved. The profession's definition guides, motivates, and affirms the determination to serve all.

The institution's definition of who the users are is the one that most directly forms the services and efforts offered. The institutional definition of user is expanded or limited by the university or college's mission, source of funding, and ever-changing mandates. Does the institution have a state directive to serve the local academic community as well as all citizens of the state? Does the mission of a private college preclude serving students from neighboring community colleges? In one institution, cooperative efforts with local high schools may be lauded and in another, adolescent researchers may be barred from entering the university library. Typically, an institution serves its students and faculty and, often less well, its staff. Are visitors of all types welcome to use the library or must they come with a letter of introduction from the dean of their college attesting to their scholarly credentials? In recent years,

many institutions have been expanding their definition of user
to include extension services participants, distance education
enrollees, private sector partners, and friends and patrons
courted by the development office.

Perhaps the most telling and legitimate definition of user
comes from the users themselves through self-selection. Are
these users only those who actually use the library or its
systems? Who are the invisible users who dial into online
catalogs? Who are those people who call asking for help in
settling a bet with the bar noise in the background? Who opts
not to be a user and why? Are the delivery systems too slow?
Does the library not have the materials they need? Should
librarians be concerned about the nonusers? Librarians would
do well to spend more time and energy determining why some
individuals become library users and why others bypass the
services and resources the profession thinks are so imperative
to academic success.

The definition of user is problematic indeed, as librarians cannot help but operate with floating and changing definitions of users. To complicate the issue further, and regardless
of which definition of user is in operation, significant demographic, social, and educational changes are altering the
composition and instructional needs of the users of academic
libraries. These agents of change have had the most visible
impact on the undergraduate population but are increasingly
reflected in the nature of graduate and faculty users. Because
undergraduate students often are the harbingers of change in
higher education, the remainder of this paper focuses primarily
on this group of users.

How Have Undergraduate Users Changed
In the Past Ten Years?

The undergraduate student of 1990 is different from the undergraduate of 1980 in a variety of ways. Significant changes in the demographics of the United States, accelerated advances in technology and its general availability, educational mandates, and social transformations have combined to produce an undergraduate population not only statistically but fundamentally different from the students of ten years ago.

Demographic Changes

Of all the transitions concurrently taking place over the past decade, none is more important than the dramatic shifts in the composition of the nation's population. For those involved in higher education, these shifts are reflected in the declining numbers of the total traditional college-age population (eighteen to twenty-four years old), increased commitment to enrolling minority students, and the influx of international students to universities and colleges.

Decreasing Traditional College Age Pool

In 1986, the Baby Boom ran out of spark as far as higher education was concerned. Americans born between 1946 and 1964 are known as the Baby Boomers. If the average Boomer born in 1964 entered college at eighteen years old and graduated four years later, he or she would have received a diploma in 1986. With the Boomers exiting the hallowed halls, a new class of students known as the Baby Busters (those born between 1965 and 1975) began filling up the lecture halls. According to Anderson et al. (1986, 3), the traditional college-age population stood at twenty-eight million; by 1990, this group decreased to twenty-six million.

Demographers sent up a red flag to university admission officers with their predictions that the decreasing college age pool would necessitate a decrease in college enrollments and ultimately in the closing of some institutions of higher education. University administrators responded to this red flag by targeting individuals outside of the traditional college age pool-- the older student. Anderson et al. goes on to say that in 1985, of the 12.2 million college students, 5.1 million or 42 percent were over the age of twenty-five years, a 24 percent increase in the number of those twenty-five and older attending college compared to ten years earlier. This new nontraditional student came to the university with different experiences, motivations, learning styles, educational demands, personal obligations, and financial situations.

In the world of stereotypes, the undergraduate enters the university at eighteen and graduates four years later at twenty-two. Increasingly, this stereotype no longer has any basis given the large number of students who attend school part-time while holding down a job or balancing family obligations. In 1986, about 57 percent of all students attended college full-time while the remaining 43 percent attended on a part-time basis. It is interesting to break down these statistics further into four-year and two-year institutions. About 70 percent of those enrolled at four-year institutions attended on a full-time basis. Anderson states that almost the opposite is true at two-year colleges where 66 percent attended on a part-time basis.

Minority Enrollments

During the 1980s, institutions of higher learning carried out minority recruitment and retention programs prompted by population shifts, administrative and federal mandates, and a desire to move toward a multicultural university.

As the nation begins the new decade, the population growth is at an historic low point. Estrada (1988, 14) points out that twenty-one million women were in the prime childbearing ages of twenty to twenty-nine years old. Yet the rate of childbirths per woman hovers around 1.8 births compared to 3.7 births at the peak of the Baby Boom. These figures reflect the overall downward trend in the fertility rate over the past twenty years in the United States. Estrada goes on to say, however, that minority groups represent a crosscurrent to the overall decline with a growth rate of two to fourteen times greater than those for the nonminority population:

> A population pyramid for the U.S. as a whole has a "top-heavy" shape, reflecting both lower fertility and the greying of America as the baby-boomer cohorts age, pushing the median age upward. But a population pyramid for a minority population has a "skyscraper" shape, with a narrow top and a broad bottom reflecting its youthfulness and expanding growth.

Despite the growing minority population, minority students are not represented proportionally in higher education enrollments. Black and Hispanic students account for 23 percent of the traditional college age population. However, according to Anderson et al. (1990, 5) only 10.4 percent of college students are Black or Hispanic. Blacks and Hispanics are not represented proportionately in enrollments challenging educators to question why some minority students still seemingly are disenfranchised from higher education.

Administrative and federal mandates for the recruitment and retention of increasing numbers of minority students have their historical basis in the educational and social upheaval of the 1960s. Universities and colleges began setting up programs to target, enroll, and graduate students who had been historically excluded from higher education. Some universities have been successful in increasing the numbers of minority students but overall there are some distressing trends with respect to black students. Between 1980 and 1986, Anderson points out that blacks as a percentage of total enrollment decreased from 9.2 percent to 8.6 percent.

One university that seems to be further along in the evolution toward a multicultural university is the University of California at Berkeley. Duckett's (1988, 168) demographic data show that in the fall of 1987, entering Berkeley freshmen were 39 percent white, 24 percent black or Hispanic, and 28.4 percent Asian American. In a 1990 conversation with Janice Koyama, at the time titled Acting Assistant Provost for Letters and Sciences, this author was told that for the first time in 1988, Berkeley's enrollments and the state of California kindergarten through twelfth grade enrollments were over 50 percent non-European whites.

International Students

Over the past decade, international students have had an increased presence on university campuses and in academic libraries. Zikopoulos' (1990, 6) report documents that in the year 1978-1979, 263,938 international students were enrolled at colleges and universities in the United States. In 1988-1989, 366,354 international students were attending colleges. She goes on to report that beginning with the post-World War II initiatives to open the doors to American universities, the number of international students enrolled has increased over one hundred fold.

A U.S. education is seen as a desirable commodity throughout the world especially in nations whose systems of higher education, research facilities, and technological knowledge are not as evolved or readily available. It is not surprising that international students have filled the classes left vacant by the Baby Bust, given the desirability and relative affordability of a U.S. degree coupled with governmental and institutional incentives.

Zikopoulos' data show that in addition to the significant increase in the numbers of international students, shifts have occurred in the country of origin as the following chart illustrates:

	International Students by World Region of Origin (Percentage of Total)						
	Africa	Asia	Europe	Latin America	Middle East	North America	Oceania
78/79	12.9	29.1	8.2	15.6	26.6	5.9	1.6
88/89	7.2	52.2	11.7	12.3	11.0	4.6	1.0

Two changes stand out: 1) the greatly increased percentage of students from Asia, and 2) the decreased percentage of students from the Middle East. Zikopoulos goes on to point out that at some universities and colleges, international students represent a greater percentage of students than even the overall minority student enrollment in the United States.

Technological Change

The undergraduate student of 1990 comes from the first generation raised in what Toffler (1981) called the "electronic cottage" with its microcomputers, video cassette recorders (VCR), car phones, modems, and walkmans. According to the *Statistical Abstract of the United States, 1989* (1990), by 1981, 2.1 million personal computers were in use. In 1987, 19.9 million microcomputers were in use. Likewise in 1981, 180 thousand modems were in use; by 1988, 8.9 million modems were linking individuals with networks and remote databases. In 1980, 1.1 percent of American households had a VCR; in 1986 the percentage had skyrocketed to 58.1 percent.

This accelerated change in the use of and availability of technology in the American home has altered user expectations of libraries. The typical undergraduate of 1990 comes to the library at least somewhat conversant in microcomputers, knowledgeable about Compuserve, and accustomed to receiving information through images. The high school graduation gift of today is no longer the typewriter or the set of luggage but a microcomputer complete with a modem. Unlike the student of 1980, most students today view the computer as a labor-saving device, something to be exploited and not to be feared. Some students do, however, attribute almost supernatural powers to the computer and expect the library's computers to link all knowledge together. Randall Hensley (1988), in a comical, tongue-in-cheek look at technology-induced behaviors in libraries, identified six prevailing undergraduate behaviors: 1) undergraduates embrace and love technology without qualification; 2) they have become impatient with using print sources, even when they are better or the only available source; 3) undergraduates like to work together when using information technologies; 4) they believe anything that comes from a

computer as if it were an oracle; 5) undergraduates have
memory loss when it comes to using print sources, often
forgetting how to use a printed index; and 6) they expect
computers to give them instant answers.

Educational Mandates

The 1980s can easily be labelled the decade of the
educational report as myriad proclamations and white papers
called for reform of the nation's educational system. At the
heart of most of these reports was the concern that schools
were not educating students in either the basics or in the ability
to function in or contribute to a rapidly changing world. In this
changing world, skills and information become quickly dated,
making it difficult to know what should be taught. What
educators agree on is that students can no longer be expected
to master a finite set of skills and knowledge to be considered
an educated person. Education reformers, business leaders,
librarians, and futurists all have called for faculty to teach
students how to learn so that learning becomes a dynamic, life-
long process. The U.S. National Commission on Excellence in
Education (1983) called for the creation of a learning society in
its report, *A Nation at Risk*:

> At the heart of such a society is the commitment
> to a set of values and to a system of education
> that affords all members the opportunity to
> stretch their minds to full capacity, from early
> childhood through adulthood, learning more as
> the world itself changes. Such a society has as a
> basic foundation the idea that education is impor-
> tant not only because of what it contributes to

one's career goals but also because of the value
it adds to the general quality of one's life.

The 1980s also saw the swell in concern for the nation's
illiteracy problem. Lori Arp (1990) points out that while much
of the concern centered around what has been called functional
illiteracy, the lack of reading and writing skills necessary to
function in the marketplace, there has been growing discussion
of literacy being relative to the changing needs of a society.
George Muñoz (1991, 464), former president of the Chicago
Board of Education, challenges librarians to reexamine their
focus on functional literacy and broaden their concern to what
he calls intellectual literacy. In the current debate, Muñoz
cautions that:

> Our concern for the fate of literacy should not be
> focused solely on the functional illiterate. Tech-
> nology will rescue them from having to learn to
> read. But what technology cannot do, nor should
> we allow it to do, is the development of our
> thinking capacity. To analyze. To think for
> ourselves.

Societal Changes

The student entering the library today has lived his or
her formative years in a world that has undergone profound
social changes. These changes are most obvious in the family
structure, the increasingly information-based economy, national
and global interdependence, and the accelerated pace of
change.

Family Structure

American families have undergone fundamental changes as the nation has responded to evolving technologies, economic conditions, and social transformations. James R. Wetzel (1990, 4), director of the Center for Demographic Studies at the U.S. Bureau of Census, describes families as the quintessential institution of the nation:

> providing both biological and social continuity as they simultaneously shape, and are shaped by, the larger society. Families also are the focus of consumption, savings, and some production activities that are vital to our overall economic well-being, and they bear special responsibilities for nurturing and educating the Nation's future work force, a critical function that is not well-served by the deterioration of the nuclear family over the past 25 or more years.

Today, fewer students than ever come from the traditional nuclear family. Wetzel (1990, 10) goes on to say that the family household is more dynamic and heterogeneous than in earlier generations. Family networks now often include former spouses and former in-laws, stepchildren, and as life expectancy increases, different generations. The family has undergone a radical transformation from 1950 when 88 percent of all households were married couple households and 11 percent of family homes were maintained by a single parent. In 1988, married couple households represented 79 percent of all homes and 20.8 were headed by single parents.

Much national discussion has centered around the growth in single-parent families. Many factors have contributed to such families including the increased rate of divorce and the greater number of unmarried mothers. Wetzel (1990, 14) states that educators are concerned that one in five children born out-of-wedlock is statistically destined to live in poverty.

Information-Based Economy

Undergraduates of 1990 are products of the information-based, knowledge-based, or postindustrial society--as these eras are often labeled. Students have grown up in a society where the majority of work is based on services, communications, and information. To be simplistic, society has evolved from one that rewarded brawn to one that now needs more brains.

Educators and business leaders agree that jobs now demand different skills and abilities than ten years ago. In this information society, Steve Benjamin (1989, 9) stresses that individuals must:

> Be able to think critically, uncover bias and propaganda, reason, question, inquire, use the scientific process, remain intellectually flexible, think about complex systems, think holistically, think abstractly, be creative, and view and read critically.

Students live in a world in which information increases geometrically and no one person can expect to keep pace with it. Students have seen their parents make career changes, go back to school for retraining after their jobs have become obsolete, and struggle to learn new computer systems. These students know nothing other than the information society.

National and Global Interdependence

The world is shrinking seemingly daily as artificial barriers dissolve before the television viewer's eyes. Advances in communication technology, microelectronics, and transportation have allowed the peoples of the world to move metaphorically closer together. Few could watch the Berlin Wall being toppled or Chinese students in the United States faxing information to protestors in Tiananmen Square to avoid the official news blackout and not marvel at how technology had indeed made the world an electronic village. As Capra (1982, 19) wrote, "We live in a globally interconnected world, in which biological, psychological, social, and environmental phenomena are all interdependent."

Accelerated Pace of Change

Change has always been inevitable but never has the world operated at the accelerated pace it does today. As historian Arthur M. Schlessinger (1986, 20) wrote, "this cumulative increase in the rate of change has been the decisive factor in the making of the modern world."

Futurists such as Alvin Toffler (1981) and John Naisbitt (1982) have repeatedly described this snowballing change and its effect on the psyche of the nation. The undergraduate of 1990 has known nothing but change and seems to thrive in such an environment--not clinging nostalgically to a time he or she never knew when the pace was slower and life was simpler.

Who Will the Users Be In the Year 2000?

Over the past decade, undergraduates have changed significantly and there is every indication that these changes will become more pronounced in the next ten years. The trends point to an increasingly multicultural student body, greater global interdependence, a growing number of invisible users, and increasing demands of a information society.

Multicultural Student Body

As the general population of the United States continues to become increasingly multicultural, so will the group of undergraduate users. Howard Fullerton (1989, 4) states that the traditional population of those eighteen to twenty-four years old from which colleges and universities draw their students will decrease from an estimated 22.5 million in 1988 to 22.4 million in 2000, representing a negative 0.4 percentage change. However, according to Estrada (1988, 18), eighteen to twenty-four year old Hispanics and Blacks will increase from 5.2 million to 6.6 million over the same period. Given the declining overall pool of college-age individuals, admission committees will be selecting their freshman classes from an increasingly multicultural pool of applicants.

The increasing numbers of minority children have already had an impact on the nation's elementary schools. Schools have responded to their increased numbers with the development of bilingual education programs, developmental and remedial education, greater emphasis on pluralism in curricular content, and multicultural teaching methods. Higher education would do well to study these responses as it prepares for the increasing numbers of minority enrollees.

A sizeable gap exists between the number of minority high school graduates and college attendees. Among Black students the gap is 54 percent and among Hispanics the gap sits at 48 percent. Estrada (1988, 19) goes on to say that not all students want or need to go to college, but:

The large number of high school graduates who are non-college bound can be seen as a latent pool that college and universities have been unable to tap successfully. It should be regarded as a high-priority pool, from which rapid inroads could be made to improve minority representation.

Colleges and universities will also be drawing from the changing immigrant population. Prior to 1960, immigrants to the United States came predominately from Germany, Italy, Canada, the United Kingdom, Poland, USSR, Hungary, and Austria. Since 1970, immigrants have traveled primarily from Mexico, the Philippines, Korea, Vietnam, Cuba, India, China, and Jamaica. Half of all immigrants now living in the United States are from Mexico, Latin America, or an Asian country and most of them have crossed the borders within the last ten years. By far the most significant immigrant group is Hispanic.

Global Interdependence

The interdependence of nations will continue to be an important economic and social influence as the century mark is reached. Several events will dramatically change the world's economic configuration in the next two years. Europe will form a new economic coalition that will make the United States the number two economic power in the world. The Pacific Rim countries, led by Japan, will increasingly exert economic power in the global market. The dismantling and reconstructing of the economic and political structures of the former Eastern Bloc countries will add to the disappearance of national economies. These new configurations point to a new framework based on global interdependence.

Pollster Louis Harris (1990, 37) provides an example of global interdependence in describing the Ford Motor Company:

> Ford Motor Company today is the prototype of what major American companies will be like by the year 2001. Ford will produce 40 percent of its cars in the Far East, 40 percent in the United States, and 20 percent in Europe. All the planning, conceptualization, production, marketing, and servicing will be done in five separate and self-contained centers, with two each located in Asia and the United States and the other in Europe.

To be able to function in such a world, the undergraduate entering the workforce in 2001 will need to develop a global perspective, cross-cultural communication skills, and an understanding of multiple cultures.

Invisible Users

With availability of telecommunication networks, an expanded computer hardware base, and an ever increasing number of online catalogs and databases accessible through remote access, an increasing number of users will become invisible users. Patricia McCandless (1985, 2) and other researchers at the University of Illinois at Urbana-Champaign described these users as the "users of information and library resources through remote electronic channels."

McCandless et al. (1985, 1) conducted the first large-scale assessment of invisible users to ascertain who they were and whether users of computer-based systems had different needs and expectations for library services than individuals who used the library on-site. The study revealed that while invisible users were fairly traditional in their methods of accessing information, they were finding ways to access information without using the library as an intermediary. Invisible users in the study were enthusiastic about seeing remote services expanded.

More recently, Sally Wayman Kalin (1989) reported on her experience with invisible users dialing into Pennsylvania State University's integrated online catalog LIAS (Library Information Access System). Kalin draws the picture of an invisible user who is older than the typical on-site user, finding many to be retired faculty. Thirty percent of the persons accessing LIAS remotely had no direct university affiliation (i.e., were not students, faculty, or staff members). Invisible users tend to be occasional users with high expectation for service. They prefer a customer/business relationship when seeking assistance in solving search and hardware problems.

The anticipated increase in invisible users over the next ten years raises some important questions. Will librarians know who they are? Will they be new users or just traditional users accessing information through electronic avenues? Who will provide the support and instruction for these users? And who will be the advocates for this growing clientele?

Increasing Demands of the Information Society

The users at the turn of the century will feel the increased demands from an information society to learn how to learn. The ability to continually learn will be essential for success in an environment that is ever changing. Users will need life-long learning skills, critical thinking abilities, and information seeking strategies.

Life-long Learning

In an information society where skills and knowledge are quickly dated, education will not end with the bestowing of a diploma. Education will become more of a life-long enterprise. It is estimated that many of the users will have three or four distinct careers during their work life. It will not be unusual for individuals to step in and out of the educational system throughout their lives.

Critical Thinking

One of the increased demands on users will be the ability to sort through and evaluate the millions of bits of information constantly bombarding them from mass media, print sources, and conversation. Individuals in an information society cannot be successful without the ability to make good decisions about their consumption of information. Critical reflective and reasonable thinking, focused on deciding what to believe or how to act, will be a vital intellectual survival skill.

Information Seeking

In an information society, knowing how to retrieve information, as opposed to having physical access to or ownership of information, will be the mark of an educated person. Knowing how to find information for personal and work use will determine if one succeeds or fails in an information society. Users will be faced with an increasingly complex society predicated on information as power. To be personally empowered, users will need sophisticated information management skills.

Changing Users: Implications For
Bibliographic Instruction

Users and their instructional needs have changed dramatically in the last ten years and will continue to evolve as the new century approaches. Some consideration must be given to whether or not current teaching methods, learning goals, and instructional programs need to be revised to fit the needs of the changing users. Given the demographic shifts in the library's population, the impact of information and instructional technologies, and the increasing demands of an information society, bibliographic instruction practitioners are faced with the responsibility to develop reasoned and appropriate responses to these new challenges. These challenges suggest four major programmatic responses for bibliographic instruction: 1) instructional emphasis, 2) instructional methods, 3) multicultural learners, and 4) equal access to information.

Instructional Emphasis

From its early focus on library orientation, bibliographic instruction has evolved on a continuum that has been influenced by changing users, evolving library environments, and an increased understanding of how individuals learn. Perhaps one of the most significant developments of the 1970s and 1980s was the shift away from tool-based to concept-based instruction. Librarians such as Kohl and Wilson (1986) found that users learned transferable information skills more readily when using conceptual frameworks and a cognitive approach to research skills instruction. The foundation laid by the first generation of bibliographic instruction librarians provides a firm ground on which to stand as the second generation looks forward to a future in which information handling skills will become even more problematic yet crucial in this world of information overload.

Consider that more libraries are expanding their online catalogs to include the likes of periodical indices, locally developed databases, and electronic bulletin boards. These "supercatalogs" bring together sources of information once physically separate. As students confront such a magic machine, will they embrace it blindly, understand its scope and limitations, walk away overwhelmed, or avoid it altogether? In order to cope with the overwhelming information choices the supercatalogs will offer, users need to be provided with a coping mechanism through teaching of critical thinking skills. Bodi (1988), Engeldinger (1988), and Oberman (1991) are among the authors who would be good sources of information about teaching critical thinking skills. Increasingly, bibliographic instruction librarians will be involved with teaching students how to make informed decisions in an information intense environment.

Instructional Methods

The changing users and evolving information environment suggest the need to explore new learning techniques and utilize technology for instructional benefit.

Learning Techniques. In order to teach the critical thinking skills that are so fundamental to coping in a world of information excess, bibliographic instruction librarians would do well to utilize active and independent learning techniques that are effective in teaching these higher level cognitive skills.

In presenting the essence of active learning, Deborah Fink (1989, 3), in her book *Process and Politics in Library Research*, calls to mind the ancient proverb, "Tell me, I forget.

Show me, I remember. Involve me, I understand." Active learning demands that students participate in the process of learning by doing, not passively listening to a library lecture. In active learning, students are given more autonomy and power over choice.   Active learning shifts the responsibility for learning to the individual and can stimulate abstract thinking, the essence of critical evaluation.

Personalized learning is based on the belief that students are heterogeneous learners and that their differences are to be recognized and embraced. As Combs (1981, 372) wrote:

> For 150 years, we have been trying to teach students as though they were alike. We have grouped them, tracked them, grade-leveled them, and tried to homogenize and organize them into one kind of group or another for administrative expedience.

Personalized education emphasizes learning goals according to individual abilities and without artificial time schedules. Personalized learning becomes even more crucial for bibliographic instruction librarians as the library and information skills of the entering undergraduates vary widely given their diverse backgrounds, variant exposure to information handling, and divergent experiences with technology.

Technology for Instructional Benefit. While it is difficult to predict which emerging instructional technologies will live up to their press releases, it is safe to say that bibliographic instruction librarians will need to increasingly exploit these technologies. Instructional technology at its best will enhance communication of information and understanding in the learning process.

Already in development and wide-spread use are interactive video systems, a technology that promotes both active and personalized learning techniques. Development of nonlinear software such as hypertext has already had an impact in encouraging instruction librarians to author computer-assisted-instruction packages not possible with earlier software. While still in relative infancy, expert systems hold promise for applying artificial intelligence techniques in teaching information evaluation skills.

The macro trends in computer technology and linkages point to an increasing student use of campus, local, regional, and national information networks. Libraries are building supercatalogs with gateway interfaces (software designed to guide the user in the selection and use of multiple databases and options) stored on increasingly powerful microcomputer workstations. The software advances in the next years will include refinements and enhancements in artificial intelligence, expert systems, natural language processing, user interfaces, and hypermedia capabilities.

Emerging instructional technologies and their appropriate use may allow bibliographic instruction librarians to actively involve students in making judicious use of the burgeoning information sources and points of access made possible through advances in computer software and hardware.

Multicultural Learners

As the user populations become increasingly multicultural, instruction practitioners will be teaching classrooms of diverse learners. Diversity in learners is nothing new in libraries, but it seems that librarians only recently have acknowledged and responded to learners as a heterogeneous population. Too often library instruction programs have been designed with the generic student in mind. The notion of a heterogeneous student body with diverse learning styles becomes even more important as users become increasingly pluralistic. With expanding diversity, there is a need for increased sensitivity in the selection of teaching styles.

Educational research such as that of B. R. Singh (1987) shows a relationship between cognitive style (field-dependency and field-independency), learning style, and culture. If members of some cultures tend to be more field-dependent, while persons of other cultures lean toward field-independency, then there are implications in teaching students from multiple cultures. The predominant mode of instruction in American universities is designed for the field-independent learner--the individual who is able to perceive items as discrete from the organized whole. The style of field-dependent learners, which studies have shown relate to Mexican and Asian cultures, may be in conflict with the style on which the teaching is based. Singh's research and its relationship to bibliographic instruction is discussed in an interesting article by Patrick Andrew Hall (1991). Bibliographic instruction librarians must recognize that they need to develop instruction that allows all learners to learn. Librarians should assume that students with different cognitive and learning styles will be enrolled along side one another in the increasingly pluralistic universities. Through concern and sensitivity and by using a variety of teaching styles, no learner needs to be put at a disadvantage.

Cultural background is but one determinant in learning style preference. As an increasing number of older students appear in the classrooms, librarians will need to further consider parallel teaching methods. Malcolm Knowles (1968, 351) began the discussion of andragogy (teaching of adults) as different from pedagogy (teaching of children) thirty years ago. Research suggests that older individuals learn differently than their younger classmates in that they are autonomous and independent learners. Bibliographic instruction librarians should heed Knowles' advice to develop instruction for the older learner that is predicated on the learner's need to be treated as an independent, self-directed individual. Tomaiuolo's (1990) review of how andragogy applies to bibliographic instruction may also be of interest to librarians.

Equal Access to Information

Perhaps the greatest issue facing bibliographic instruction librarians over the next ten years is how equal access to information can be safeguarded. In a society where information denotes economic, political, and personal power, equal access to that information is fundamental to individual empowerment and equality. Teaching students how to access, evaluate, and use information becomes an increasingly political act. By teaching users how to navigate in this information intense world, librarians can help to safeguard equal access to information.

Yet, with access to information increasingly dependent on technology (i.e., networks, modems, computers, printers), individuals who are "technology have-nots" are disenfranchised in an information society. Librarians need to take a leadership role in seeing that all individuals have access to necessary hardware and attendant instruction in and support of its use.

In addition to the inequities created by lack of necessary technology, computers create psychological and educational barriers for some of the users. A sizeable body of research by authors such as Clark et al. (1989) and Cardman (1990) supports the perception that in the area of computer use, there exists a gender gap. With the advent of online catalogs, CD-ROM periodical databases, and now supercatalogs, libraries may inadvertently be providing access that is biased toward male users. What role can bibliographic instruction librarians play in addressing this gender gap? As Clark et al., (1989, 117), have suggested:

Simple, yet effective measures might include:

1) Targeting females as a group needing different instruction. The notion of singling out females may seem to smack of sexism but bibliographic instruction practitioners have long acknowledged that library users have diverse instructional needs and have in response developed differentiated programs for international students, disadvantaged students, disabled patrons, and gifted students. We must be aware that there are various learning styles and preferences. Why not develop programs especially for women designed to address their previous experience with computers, their preferred learning style, and their mental models of computers?

2) Eliminating sexist computer practices. Refrain from asking only males to demonstrate computer use or serve as computer assistants. During instruction sessions, target female students in the group. Ask a female to assist in demonstration, thereby providing a subtle role model for the other women in the group. Avoid scheduling computer use on a first-come, first-served basis; males usually get there first. Avoid using "he" for the generic computer user; use "they" or "he" or "she" equally.

3) Making computer use as social as possible. According to Sanders, (1986) women have exhibited a preference for learning to use computers in pairs or trios. Learning situations which emphasize group interaction and exchange are more effective with women than tutorial or programmed instruction. Create an environment which is welcoming and non-threatening to women. Librarians can begin by surveying the physical configuration of computers and workstations. Because women prefer to work in pairs or trios, arranging at least some computers in clusters or semi-circles will encourage group interaction and facilitate learning.

4) Stressing the importance of using the computer to access information during the course of instruction. Since women prefer to use systems in a task oriented context rather than exploring the potential of the system, they need to be introduced to the range of capabilities of the system which they then could apply to their tasks. Otherwise, women may rely on interfaces and simple search strategies rather than develop sophisticated search skills which would allow them to utilize the full potential of online catalogs and electronic bibliographic databases.

Perhaps most important, instruction librarians need to conduct research on computer use by all learners, not just females, to identify the presence and magnitude of any other gaps that might be developing as libraries increasingly depend on technology for access to information. Librarians need to increase their advocacy role in safeguarding that technology becomes the equalizer not the unequalizer in information access.

Conclusion

Over the past ten years, users of academic libraries, and in particular undergraduates, have changed significantly. Due to dramatic shifts in the nation's demographics, the undergraduate population is more pluralistic, drawing increasingly from minority groups, immigrant sectors, international students, and older learners. These users have grown up in a technologically intense environment and their increased expectations of libraries reflect this. They are from the first generation who has lived its childhood in Toffler's electronic cottage. Students come from households that are more dynamic and heterogeneous than in earlier generations. They live in a world where information increases geometrically and no one can "get a handle on it," where nations are interdependent, and where accelerating change is the norm. Users no longer need to come through the library doors to search for information; they are increasingly invisible as they remotely access libraries. The student of 1990 is made from different cloth than the freshman of 1980. These changed learners pose new challenges for bibliographic instruction librarians. The changing users and their evolving needs demand that bibliographic instruction librarians emphasize teaching the critical thinking skills that will enable students to succeed in a world of information overload; that active learning, personalized learning, and instructional technology be used to the student's benefit, that consideration be given to multicultural learners; and, perhaps most important, that through teaching information retrieval and critical use, bibliographic instruction librarians can help safeguard equal access to information for all users.

References

Anderson, Charles et al., compilers. 1990. *Fact book on higher education (1989-1990)*. New York: American Council on Education and Macmillan Publishing Co.

Arp, Lori. 1990. "Information literacy or bibliographic instruction: Semantics or philosophy?" *RQ* 30 (Fall): 46-49.

Benjamin, Steve. "An ideascape for education: What futurists recommend," *Educational Leadership*. 47 (September): 9.

Bodi, Sonia. 1988. "Critical thinking and bibliographic instruction: The relationship," *Journal of Academic Librarianship*. 14 (July): 150-153.

Capra, Fritjof. 1982. "The turning point: A new vision of reality," *The Futurist*. 16 (June): 19.

Cardman, Elizabeth R. 1990. "The gender gap in computer use: Implications for BI," *Research Strategies*. 8 (Summer): 116-128.

Clark, Barton M., et al. 1989. "Gender gap in the use of library technologies: Evidence, implications and intervention." In *Building on the first century: Proceedings of the fifth national conference of the association of college and research libraries*. Chicago: Association of College Research Libraries.

Combs, Arthur W. 1981. "What the future demands of education," *Phi Delta Kappan* 62 (May): 372.

Duckett, Willard. 1988. "An Interview with Harold Hodgkinson: using demographic data for long-range planning," *Phi Delta Kappan* 70 (October): 168.

Engeldinger, Eugene. 1988. "Bibliographic instruction and critical thinking: The contribution of the annotated bibliography," *RQ* 28 (Winter): 195-202.

Estrada, Leobardo. 1988. "Anticipating the demographic future," *Change* 20 (May/June): 14, 18-19.

Fink, Deborah. 1989. *Process and politics in library research.* Chicago: American Library Association.

Fullerton, Howard N., Jr. 1986. "New labor force projections, spanning 1988 to 2000," *Monthly Labor Review.* 112 (November): 4.

Hall, Patrick Andrew. 1991. "Relationship as pedagogy: The role of affectivity in instructing people of color: Some implications for bibliographic instruction," *Library Trends*, (Winter): 316-326.

Harris, Louis. 1990. "2001: The world our students will enter," *Independent School.* 49 (Winter): 37.

Hensley, Randall. 1988. "CD-ROM users and technology-induced behavior." Unpublished paper presented at the American Library Association, New Orleans, LA. 10 July.

Kalin, Sally Wayman. 1989. "Invisible user/visible technology."
    Unpublished paper presented at the American Library
    Association, Dallas, TX. 25 June.

Knowles, Malcolm. 1968.   "Andragogy not pedagogy!" *Adult
    Leadership.* 16 (April): 351.

Kohl, David F., and Lizabeth A. Wilson. 1986. "Effectiveness
    of course-integrated bibliographic instruction in improv-
    ing coursework," *RQ* 27 (Winter): 206-211.

Koyama, Janice, Acting Assistant Provost for Letters and
    Sciences, University of California at Berkeley. 1990.
    Interview by author. 14 June.

McCandless, Patricia, et al. 1985. *The invisible user: User needs
    assessment for library public services.*   University of
    Illinois, Final Report from Public Services Research
    Projects sponsored by the General Electric Foundation.
    Washington, DC: Office of Management Studies, Associ-
    ation of Research Libraries.

Muñoz, George. 1991. "Literacy in the twenty-first century,"
    Illinois Libraries. 73 (May): 163-164.

Naisbitt, John. 1982. *Megatrends: Ten new directions transform-
    ing our lives.* New York: Warner Books.

Oberman, Cerise. 1991.   "Avoiding the cereal syndrome or
    critical thinking in the electronic environment," *Library
    Trends.* 39 (Winter). 189-202.

Sanders, Jo Shuchat. 1986. "Closing the computer gap," *Education Digest*. 52 (October): 22-23.

Schlesinger, Arthur M., Jr. 1986. "The challenge of change," *New York Times Magazine*. 27 July, 20.

Singh, B.R. 1987. "Cognitive styles, cultural pluralism and effective teaching and learning," *International Review of Education*. 34: 355-370.

Statistical Abstract of the United States 1989. 1990. Washington, DC: Government Printing Office.

Toffler, Alvin. 1981. *The third wave*. New York: Bantam Books.

Tomaiuolo, Nicholas G. 1990. "Reconsidering bibliographic instruction for adult reentry students: Emphasizing the practical," *RSR* (Spring): 49-54.

U.S. National Commission on Excellence in Education. 1983. *Anation at risk: The imperative for educational reform: A report to the nation and the secretary of education*. Washington, DC: Government Printing Office.

Wetzel, James R. 1990. "American families: 75 years of change," *Monthly Labor Review* 113 (March): 4-12.

Zikopoulos, Marianthi. 1990. *Open doors 1988/89: Report on international educational exchange*. New York, Institute of International Education.

THE CHANGING USER AND THE FUTURE OF BIBLIO-GRAPHIC INSTRUCTION: A PERSPECTIVE FROM THE HEALTH SCIENCES LIBRARY

James Shedlock

Introduction

From the perspective of the librarian, the changing user presents demanding challenges and opportunities to professionals engaged in "information management education"--a phrase common to many academic health sciences librarians that is synonymous with the phrase "bibliographic instruction." These challenges deal with the problem of addressing change--change in user behavior, change in user needs, and change in user perception about the library and the information environment with which he or she interacts on a daily basis. Evaluating how effectively librarians address these changes provides an opportunity for professional self-reflection.

Librarians look for challenges in the concept of the changing user because, like their users, librarians also change. In fact, librarians want change. Librarians change in relation to their users, and these changes are based upon how librarians perceive their users' information needs. The first challenge implicit in the concept of the changing user is to the profession, one that seeks new direction for the future of the information management education discipline in academic libraries. The second challenge is to academic health sciences librarians: (a)

What is the health sciences librarian's role within academic librarianship's service goal of teaching the user how to access information? and (b) What can health sciences librarians contribute from their own unique experiences toward understanding the importance of the library's teaching mission? This essay attempts to address the first challenge by reflecting on its importance through the second challenge.

Health sciences librarians have much to share with their academic colleagues. The health sciences disciplines themselves all offer distinct characteristics for the way information is created, used, organized, controlled, and disseminated. Health sciences information results from concentrated research that expands the knowledge base of biomedicine while attempting to solve the complex mysteries of human disease. Health sciences information must be timely in dissemination to individual users. Hence, the interest in and emphasis on electronic access to biomedical information, the traditional reliance on the journal format, and the importance of resource sharing among health sciences libraries. Starting with this perspective, academic health sciences librarians have been forming a vision of their future within the academic health sciences center and with their users. This vision relies upon new uses of technology to alter what librarians do for users; it redefines the role of librarians in relation to their users; and it stresses the importance of information management within health sciences professional education.

The ideas expressed here focus on the direction that health sciences libraries are taking in information management education. The basis for the thoughts and ideas to follow stem from the following three questions:

1) Who are the library's users, and how can they be identified?

2)   How have user populations changed over the
past ten years?
3)   Finally, do remote access services create a
new user population, and if so, how can information management education respond to their
needs?

Generally, these questions revolve around the concept of the
changing user. In addition, it is important to reflect on how
librarians have adapted to the changing user and what further
adaptations lie ahead.

Who Are the Library's Users?

As Lizabeth Wilson points out in another chapter of this
book, a number of factors influence those who are potential
recipients of bibliographic instruction.   These influences
include: the library profession's definition of the user; the
institution's policies about who receives library services; and the
user's own definition or self-recognition of the need for library
instruction. While these three definitions are valid, the health
sciences librarian sees them from a unique viewpoint.   In
addition, the question, "Who are the library's users?" cannot
simply be entertained as a rhetorical exercise, but must be
viewed as an opportunity to reach out and understand users'
specific information needs.

Professional Definition of the Library User

For the health sciences librarian, there has been less
imperative to consider every citizen a bona fide user of the
nearest available health sciences library.   Health sciences
libraries have been traditionally defined as serving professional

education, biomedical research and patient care. Thus, they are specialized and therefore naturally restrictive. This definition of the health sciences library places limits on services and information to groups unprepared to deal with the technical information intrinsic to a health sciences collection. While the need for health information and patient education increases, especially during these times of stress on the nation's health care delivery systems, and when major health problems, such as AIDS, heart disease, and substance abuse, can be attributed to behavioral causes, traditional limits on what health sciences libraries can do by way of educational services for the general public have prevailed. This may begin to change as the public exerts pressure on health sciences librarians--in public and private universities as well as in hospitals--to respond with specific health information appropriate for a more educated populace.

While collaboration with public libraries may be one way of responding to this pressure, it is conceivable that the public may turn away from its traditional source of health information--the public library--and direct its attention toward what is perceived as the ultimate, and therefore more accurate and more qualitative, source of health information, the academic or hospital health sciences library (i.e., the patient or the patient's family may want the same source of information that the physician uses). The public's need for health information may mark a trend toward extending library services, such as information management education, to the general public.

The Institution's Definition of the User

The institution's definition of user groups is the primary influence on the academic health sciences library in determining who receives library services. This definition is generally found in mission statements and goals of the university, school or library, and it is from these statements that library administrators receive guidance toward identifying user groups for the health sciences library to serve. Occasionally, new user groups are identified which result from efforts by campus leaders to reach new "markets" of students. The growth and expansion of academic programs and the arrival of new user groups on campus results from the many efforts made by campus leaders to achieve success in fulfilling the university's mission within society. Establishing innovative programs that appeal to a new body of students or acquiring, merging, or establishing contractual agreements among new institutions brings in new user groups that an academic health sciences library would automatically identify as its own, and to which it would extend the benefit of all library services including information management education. Some examples may include the medical school creating new operating agreements with formerly unaffiliated community hospitals, expanding health care delivery from the medical school to corporations or industry, or establishing joint research endeavors with professional associations, private research centers, or government agencies.

The User's Self-Identification

Some users naturally identify themselves as potential students of information management education. These users are the first to schedule appointments with librarians or register for library-sponsored programs. They value their information sources, have a desire for effective information-seeking behaviors, and acknowledge the role of libraries and librarians in the health sciences disciplines and in society. These professionals and students are eager to learn new techniques that will assist them in finding, managing and using information relevant to their work.

The Health Sciences Library's Definition of User Groups

For health sciences libraries, a literal response to the question, "Who are the library's users?", includes the same type of groups served on the academic campus: faculty, students, staff and any other affiliated users. While academic librarians will certainly recognize many of the same categories of users as those on the health sciences campus, it is important to recognize two qualitative differences between academic and health sciences user groups. First, when discussing user groups in the health sciences, librarians are generally describing professional students. The scientific nature and societal value of their discipline, the intensity of study, the rigor of the curriculum, and the goal of licensed practice within society distinguishes these students from other graduate students. A second and important distinction between the health sciences and all other disciplines is the clinical element. The health sciences list of potential "students" for information management education includes additional groups not seen on the academic campus--interns, residents, fellows, postdoctoral students, clinical faculty, administrators of healthcare institutions, various practitioners, such as nurses and allied health professionals (therapists, technicians, etc.)--whose sole educational program or connection with the university revolves around patient care. The centrality of patient care within the health care environment exerts special pressures and stresses on the delivery of information services to health sciences users and influences the delivery of educational programs. Teaching the clinically-oriented user group is an important part of the health sciences library's task in meeting its service goals. These two characteristics of health sciences user populations--the nature of their academic disciplines and the importance of patient care in professional education--shape the perspective of health sciences librarians and colors much of everything they do, especially information management education.

A specific list of health sciences user groups would include:

1)   Professional students in medicine, dentistry, nursing, pharmacy, and various allied and public health sciences. It is important to remember that all of these disciplines have subdisciplines as well.

2)   Graduate students in the basic health sciences.

3)   Interns, residents, fellows, and postdoctoral candidates.

4)   Faculty. Faculty are students in the sense of pursuing life-long education--relearning their own discipline as well as learning new subjects, such as information management principles and techniques, which directly relate to their teaching, research, and patient care activities.

5)   Researchers with faculty rank and their professional staff in all of the disciplines mentioned above.

6)   Practitioners in the same above disciplines. Practitioners are commonly known as clinical faculty holding a university appointment and who teach at the bedside. Health sciences librarians would naturally identify these practitioners as their users, and therefore should be considered a user group for educational services. Community

physicians without faculty appointment remain unaffiliated but are attracting the attention of the National Library of Medicine (NLM) as an important user group needing professional information management education. In the NLM's *Long Range Plan* (1986, 46) "developing ways to provide basic levels of information services to isolated geographic areas in which health professionals are still underserved" receives important attention.

7)   Administrators of various health care institutions affiliated with the academic medical center.

Reaching the Health Sciences User

Health sciences librarians, like their academic colleagues, define users and establish labels for various user groups only as a means of organizing their approach to providing information management education services. When health sciences librarians discuss users' information needs, especially in terms of education and training, emphasis is often placed on a familiar topic--reaching out to users. Health sciences librarians ask themselves, "Can we do more for our users? If so, how can we do more? Have we forgotten a user group? Is everyone served?" And as librarians become more experienced as teachers, other important questions arise: "What has been accomplished by these educational programs? Are users smarter as a result of our teaching? Do users exhibit or demonstrate positive behavioral change toward meeting their information needs? Are users more effective in identifying, retrieving, and evaluating information?"

Efforts to evaluate a health sciences library's education service forces librarians to ponder the issue of the user. Health sciences librarians must ask, "How do users use information? Why do they seek information? What can we teach them to help them satisfy their information needs?" Ultimately, the original question of "Who are the library's users?" is seen not in the sense of identifying institutional labels but in addressing unspoken need. The challenge in the future is to understand the user and the user's need for information and the various forms and types of information needed at different times in the user's professional career. Health sciences librarians, as well as other academic librarians, should seek out their users and establish a dialogue with them. The purpose of the dialogue is to learn. Librarians need to learn from their users who they are in terms of being information consumers and what they value as students of information management. As McCool (1989, 23) has pointed out:

> there are calls for librarians to become more active outside the library. Time must be spent talking with faculty, attending departmental faculty meetings, serving on general education and writing committees, in short, becoming more visible and selling the value of libraries and librarians.

This proactive stance is necessary "to counter the lack of understanding of the full contribution libraries and librarians can make to undergraduate and graduate education."

All academic librarians will be challenged to understand users differently as the user changes. Librarians accept the challenge because it is their professional responsibility to do so. Librarians acknowledge the need to evaluate teaching efforts continuously in order to know their users better. By emphasizing ongoing evaluation of information management education programs, librarians set up the process of identifying and recognizing their user groups.

How Can Librarians Identify User Groups?

Literally taken, this question asks for techniques in approaching user groups on campus. Some of these techniques may include: 1) using the health sciences library director's position as both a liaison and an initial contact for promoting education services; 2) establishing a formal liaison program with campus departments; and 3) watching for hints of an educational need while at the reference or information desk.

The Library Director as Liaison

Ideally, the health sciences library director is the chief liaison for all the library's services, certainly in terms of promoting services as part of the library's mission. But in identifying new user groups, the director is most likely the best person to hear of them as well as to hear expressions of unmet needs. By virtue of the position, the health sciences library director is closest to the authority that approves new user groups and to those thinking of expanding educational programs. Curriculum committee responsibilities, for example, as well as similar administrative tasks, put the library director in direct and indirect communication channels for hearing what goes on in the way of program development inside the medical center. The library director also serves as chief advocate of the library's educational role. The director is in a position to promote information management education to curriculum planners, can speak about the effect information management skills will play in the work environment of the institution's graduates, and can address the relationship between such skills and the life-long learning process. The information gleaned from various contacts defines the library's various user groups and keeps staff in tune to what is needed in the way of education services.

Establishing a Formal Liaison Program

This author reported in an earlier essay (1983, 61) about the importance of liaison programs for gathering data about what is being offered or planned in individual departments. Liaison programs generally rely on one, some, or all of the reference staff dividing up the medical center into constituent groups and reaching out to make regular contact with influential users in their respective departments, centers, or programs. Regular contact with users results in enhanced knowledge of initiatives that are projected, under development, or planned for the near future. This identification of user's needs can provide a head start in preparing educational services.

Identifying User's New Needs

Individual users are not reticent about telling health sciences librarians when and how they need help accessing information. When questions come to the reference desk that indicate both a need for instruction and a desire to learn, staff receive a strong signal that a user group requires attention. Admittedly, there is a fine line between presenting a legitimate question for information at the reference desk and implicitly demonstrating a lack of knowledge about library use. Katz (1978, 261) has said that a user should not be forced to receive instruction when all he or she wants is information. The point is that users do offer insights into what they need to know about library use and that this need could be remedied by an educational program or two. Once a potential group is identified via this method, librarians should use their investigative skills to track down influential faculty members or administrators who can assist in the promotion of library classes, orientations to new information sources, or library tours, or who are willing to incorporate information management education into their respective courses using the librarian as a team teacher.

Outreach methods, such as those described above, demonstrate examples of how librarians can reach out to users. Regardless of the approach taken, the intent is to remind users of an important library service while also providing librarians with an opportunity to investigate users' information needs. But the point here should go beyond methods. Methods in and of themselves are not that important; means of identifying users and their instructional needs will change over time. What is important is that librarians must *want* to identify users and their needs. Being proactive with users must come to be synonymous with the term and concept of "librarian". Librarians must have the attitude that allows them to be open to opportunities with users and to create such opportunities with users. By using these methods, librarians--in all disciplines--take on an active role in their users' education. A proactive stance by librarians demonstrates that they have an intrinsic role rather than a supplementary one in the mission of the university.

Marketing Information Management Education

In reaching out to users, the underlying question may really be one of how do we market or promote information management education? If that is the case, the issue of promotion and marketing challenges librarians to pay attention to what is being "sold". As Miller and Coons and Rader state in other chapters in this book, the product that librarians offer should be a service--an educational program--that helps users solve their information problems.

In marketing and promoting information management education, what is also "sold" is a better understanding and appreciation of the library as an educational resource and librarians as information professionals. Marketing and promotion of information management education services link libraries directly to the user's life-long learning process. But what will make the sale to the user? Credibility is what makes users accept the education mission of the library and the librarian. Promotion and marketing will be successful if health sciences librarians (all librarians, really) establish programs with credible staff--i.e., effective teachers--who have valid theories and sound practices to teach.

Part of the solution to the marketing problem is to have librarians who are *good* teachers. Not all librarians can or should teach. Those who can teach should be freed from other tasks to prepare their instruction. Such support is crucial to the success of the library's educational role. Those who cannot teach should not be forced to do so. McCool (1978) comments:

> However, if an individual hates teaching, is not a good teacher or is not supportive of the BI effort, s/he should not be forced to become involved. S/He may undermine the entire effort if his/her negativism spreads to the students s/he teaches and/or to his/her librarian colleagues.

Those who cannot teach because of a lack of skills but want to teach should be directed to areas where their skills can be better utilized by the library or be allowed to develop teaching skills through additional education or training.

Part of being a good teacher is having the right combination of skills and personality. Teaching skills include organizing information, presenting concepts, demonstrating techniques, devising exercises, listening and responding to students, testing for learning, and evaluating new material. Personality skills should reflect the teacher's self-confidence in his or her own knowledge of the materials presented and in the ability to convey the material with style and in a fashion where the student grasps and appreciates the concept to be learned. Personality also implies attitude, and librarians must have the attitude to teach, to want their students to learn, and find information for themselves--to be independent learners. Librarians must have the desire to be good teachers. To increase their credibility, librarians demonstrate, through their skills, using whatever opportunity presents itself, that they can teach as effectively (if not more so) and be as good as the faculty think they are. Library courses require good content to be successful (i.e., satisfying an information need), but equally important, they need and require good teachers. The challenge in the future will be for librarians to establish their credibility-- as instructors, as information specialists, and as professionals.

If information management education librarians concentrate on reaching out to their users and are mindful of identifying their user groups, then it is equally important to place these efforts within the context of the user's mindset. What is important to users in terms of information access and availability, and, how can that be translated into information management programs? Librarians must remember that what is important to users can change over time. Influences, such as the growth of information in their respective fields, the availability of information tools, the desire for assistance, and the need to incorporate new ideas into curricula, are important factors in the change process, and ones that information management education librarians must incorporate in their planning for future programs.

How Have User Populations Changed Over the Past Ten Years?

The health sciences professions provide realistic examples of how much and how fast users have changed in the past ten years. There are four areas that demonstrate the degree of change. First, health sciences users are now more knowledgeable about the value of information and the impact it has in their work. Second, health sciences users are more reliant and dependent on, as well as aware of, technology, especially the personal computer, and its potential for handling information-related work. This awareness of information technology follows from the healthcare professional's desire to use technology as a means of improving patient management or supporting biomedical research. The embrace of the personal computer as an information tool represents important evidence of change. Third, health sciences users have realized the overwhelming prospects of having to deal with a changing information environment and are willing to accept assistance in coping with the information explosion. Fourth, health sciences users are also aware of their professional obligation to relearn their field of study as well as to educate the next generation in a way that better prepares the new practitioner for an ever changing field. All of the these areas--the user's acknowledgement of the information environment, the user's dependence on technology, the user's need for assistance and guidance, and the user's awareness that learning is life-long--are interconnected with each other and influence library practice and information services.   Each of these areas is discussed in relation to the provision of information management education services.

The User's Acknowledgment of the Information Environment

Sources, such as Barnett (1989, 197) and Huth (1989, 647), explain that users know they are in the midst of a serious problem of information overload and have begun to realize how this problem has evolved over time.   Barnett writes:

> In the last two decades we have witnessed what has been labeled the "information explosion" in medical knowledge. Many medical education leaders and most students feel overwhelmed by "information overload" in conjunction with the static, passive nature of medical school.   The practice of medicine is dominated by how we process, record, retrieve and communicate information.   The explosion of knowledge in the basic medical sciences and in the development of new methods for diagnosing and treating illness makes it a formidable task to keep abreast of the medical knowledge base.   It has been estimated that over 600,000 articles are published in the biomedical literature each year.   If the most conscientious physician were to attempt to keep up with the literature by reading two articles per day, in one year even this compulsive individual would be over 800 years behind.

Hamilton (1990, 1331) points out that users have also realized how they themselves have contributed to the information explosion. In a *Science* news article, Hamilton reports research opinions and findings that:

> indicate that 55% of the papers published be-
> tween 1981 and 1985 in journals indexed by the
> institute [Institute for Scientific Information]
> received no citations at all in the 5 years after
> they were published.... Timothy Springer, a
> Harvard cancer researcher, was more direct. 'It is
> higher than I'd have expected,' he said. It indi-
> cates that too much is published. A lot of us
> think too much is published.... The obvious
> interpretation is that the publish or perish syn-
> drome is still operating in force.... In many ways,
> publication no longer represents a way of com-
> munication with your scientific peers, but a way
> to enhance your status and accumulate points for
> promotion and grants.

This awareness of an information explosion coupled with a need for and access to information represents a major change in the user's perspective of professional literature.

This new perspective impacts on information manage-
ment education services because it indicates that the user is open to solutions, namely, how education and training in the use of technology can provide skills for managing massive amounts of academic information. For example, health sciences librarians often hear decision makers, especially deans and influential faculty responsible for defining the curriculum, express their awareness of the need for better information management practices. A short-term solution is to be found in developing personal skills that will assist health care professionals in managing their individual corner of the world's biomedi-

cal knowledge base. (Education is considered a short-term solution relevant to the information explosion problem because there are a number of factors influencing the phenomenal growth and cost of scientific literature that cannot be resolved by information management education alone. Byrd (1990, 184) and Metz and Gherman (1991, 315), on the other hand, address some long-range solutions to the problem, and these go beyond teaching information management principles and skills to professionals.) The solution, from this new perspective, means two things: using the technology to its advantage as a tool for quickly processing large files of text and teaching new professionals how to use this tool for managing information. Meshing information management education with computer literacy skills provides an ideal means of assisting the changing user in coping with information overload.

The User's Interest in Technology

Technology has always played a critical role in modern healthcare. Many achievements in medicine often overshadow the use of the various technologies that brought about these same discoveries. Health care professionals are no strangers to using technology. One primary example of how health sciences professionals have changed over the past ten years is shown by their embrace of technology for doing library research, a phenomenon now identified as end-user searching. While the MEDLINE database has been popular since the mid-1970s, mostly as a tool for health sciences librarians in providing information services to their users, health sciences professionals and researchers have accepted personal online searching in large numbers. Wallingford et al. (1990, 166) report that:

the composition of the NLM's online user group
has changed.   Nearly half the passwords that
allow access to the NLM system are now assigned
to individuals as opposed to libraries or other
institutions, and the number of individual users is
growing much faster than the number of institutional users. Over the past twelve months, individual users accounted for more than one third of
the 4.5 million MEDLINE searches conducted on
the NLM system.

Kotzin and Eichenberger (1990) also report that individual
password holders account for nearly half of the total number of
passwords assigned for access to the NLM system.

Since FY 1986, the year GRATEFUL MED was
introduced, the number of codes has increased by
50% or more every year.... Most interesting is
that GRATEFUL MED users now account for
51% of the codes accessing MEDLARS databases
each month.... Moreover, when one examines the
number of search sessions each month there is a
steady increase by those using GRATEFUL
MED.

(GRATEFUL MED is an inexpensive communication software
package aimed at the end user to assist the searching of NLM
databases, notably MEDLINE.)
     The popularity of personal online searching reflects the
health professional's recognition of the need to keep up with
the literature, to integrate more of the findings cited in the
literature into their work, and to satisfy their growing interest
in computers.

Another example of how users have changed via technology is the birth of a new health science discipline: medical informatics. Medical informatics is the discipline that studies the use of computer technology in the health sciences, especially in medicine, dentistry, and nursing. As a discipline, medical informatics results from user efforts to understand the computer as a tool for use in processing information. Blois (1986, 776) points out that information is "the commodity with which informatics deals." He remarks in particular about the increased use of computers in more effective medical information management:

> the role computers are now taking on is also that of a breakthrough tool--one enabling us to explore and better understand the informational and cognitive foundations of medicine. Its application to the classification and retrieval of data and to the management of information will result in a deeper insight into the structure of medical information and knowledge itself.... The mass of unlearned or forgotten medical information has not disappeared nor has it become useless or irrelevant. Rather, what have now become necessary are better means of managing this information and locating it when needed. It is here that we have turned to computers and to information science for help. This is a major undertaking and a new adventure for medicine.

Shortliffe and Perreault (1990) state that the field of medical informatics has grown steadily in the past ten years. The arrival of a new discipline--one dedicated to finding how technology can be combined with medicine, nursing, dentistry, and all the

other health sciences professions--is testament to the changes
users have undergone.

This new medical informatics discipline is also having a
major impact on the changing curriculum. Faculty are especially aware of the need to incorporate information management
and computer literacy into the curriculum in order to meet their
goals of educating new professionals to deal with change in
their professional practice. Health sciences professionals are
looking more and more to technology as the answer to their
information management problems, and they are aware of the
need to teach the use of information technologies as early in
the curriculum as possible. Because librarians have demonstrated their knowledge of personal computers and the computer's
usefulness as a tool for managing information, they are seen by
user groups as a valued source of training and advice, especially
in tracking and searching potential databases in the health
sciences. The user's awareness both of technology's benefits
and the library's use of information technology produces a
greater interest in the library's teaching role within the medical
center.

The User's Need for Assistance and Guidance

The health sciences curricula are changing in response
to the influences noted above; namely, the expanding knowledge base in the health sciences and the importance of the
personal computer as an information management tool.
Curriculum planners within the many healthcare professions
realize the need to incorporate information management
principles and techniques into their formal educational programs. Indeed, the whole medical profession speaks definitively
on the need to change the curriculum to include instruction on
how computers can assist medicine. *Physicians for the Twenty-*

First Century, the GPEP Report (1984) describes, through a series of conclusions and recommendations, the changes needed within medical education to prepare physicians for future practice. The report "affirms that all physicians, regardless of specialty, require a common foundation of knowledge, skills, values, and attitudes." Included in this foundation are recommendations about acquiring learning skills, learning independently, and the role of information sciences. In the section on acquiring learning skills, the report stresses the need to learn independently, which can be achieved through faculty guidance of learning opportunities, through reduced scheduled time within the curriculum, and through reduced lecture hours. The report also emphasizes the incorporation of information sciences and computer technology into the general professional education of physicians and recommends designating "an academic unit for institutional leadership in the application of information sciences and computer technology." Whether or not the health sciences library is this unit, the *GPEP Report* identifies potential educational roles for librarians in the professional education of physicians.

The new curricula that are evolving are also stressing different learning styles. Students need to learn how to learn. Less emphasis is placed on learning by lecture and other passive techniques, and more emphasis should be placed on individual thinking and acquiring problem-solving skills. Burrows (1990, B1) writes:

> The solution, then, is to restructure the way in which students learn the necessary material. First, there is a core of medical information that simply must be learned.... Next, medical-school teachers need to provide a conceptual framework into which students can integrate facts as they

acquire them. Then, students must learn how to
decide what information they require for a decision.... Finally, medical students will have to be
able to gain access to but not necessarily learn,
the massive amounts of information required to
practice medicine.

Burrows also concludes that in addition to applying technology
to learning issues, there is an important need for "close
cooperation with the medical library in making use of advances
in information science." Self-directed learning is the survival
technique of the future. The whole thrust of end-user searching
is positive proof of the users' change toward and interest in
taking charge of their education and learning process.

What is the impact of these changes on information
management education? Curriculum reform provides an open
window for new opportunities on the part of health sciences
librarians. Some librarians are strategically placed on curriculum committees and can remind faculty of the librarian's role
as teacher. Those librarians not participating in curriculum
design should assert their influence and convince faculty of the
value of using librarians as teachers within their curriculum.
With the invitation extended, health sciences librarians welcome
the chance to either have a slice of the curriculum pie as their
very own or to be part of the teaching team that covers
concepts, lessons, and techniques of information management
in whatever course a willing faculty member offers. The
invitation alone would be a significant symbol of the changing
age.

The User's Awareness that Learning is Life-Long

Continuing education (CE) has been a long-standing hallmark of the health sciences professions. In many professions, especially medicine, continuing education is stipulated as mandatory for ongoing licensure or recertification. Over the past ten years there has been a growing awareness by continuing education educators that the same forces effecting change in the health sciences curriculum also impact on practitioners in the field as well. Along with this awareness is the evolution of continuing education as a concern of the health sciences librarian. Both continuing education educators and health sciences librarians are awakening to shared roles and responsibilities in order to meet the demands of clinicians who must manage their information needs using the best technology possible. Hackleman and Bischoff (1990, 155) advise librarians that:

> To meet the real CE needs of the health care practitioner, librarians and CE professionals must work closely together in the future. This cooperation will fully use their individual strengths in the areas of automation, assessment of need, and knowledge and skill transfer.

The Role of the Librarian

Users have changed significantly during the past decade. They are more aware of the personal impact the information explosion has made in their work. They are intrigued and challenged by personal computer technology as an information management tool. They have concluded that there is a need to incorporate teaching the use of information technology into the professional education curriculum. And they have looked toward the library profession as a source of education and training for learning information management principles and techniques. The changing user creates opportunities for librarians to take on new roles as teacher and consultant. As these key roles are fulfilled and skills are demonstrated through pilot projects, grant awards or through innovative experiments, librarians gain attention and respect for their accomplishments. Administrators take notice and begin to recognize the potential that librarians possess in the professional education of students, in the provision of information services within the health sciences center, and in the use of technology to solve the information explosion phenomenon. While the user has changed these past ten years, so has the librarian. Adapting to the user's new condition--an awareness of the information explosion and the impact technology can have on managing information--is a characteristic of the new librarian. Continuous adaptation to change in response to the user's educational and information needs will distinguish information management education services in the future.

When speaking of the changing user and the influence users have on a changing library profession, librarians must be mindful of off-campus users as well. This group has also changed, but perhaps at a somewhat slower pace because of the reduced availability of resources. Technology, especially advances in telecommunications, begins to close the gap between remote user groups and their access to information resources.

Do Remote Access Information Services
Create a New User Population?

If So, How Can Bibliographic Instruction
Respond To Their Needs?

Remote Access Information Services

Basically, remote access information services do not create a *new* user population. User groups were already in place before remote access information services became available. Remote access information services now provide the means to an end, namely, the delivery of information to users who need it. Information and communications technology provide a connection between the library and teaching librarians with existing user populations whose geographic separation from main campus is their only distinguishing characteristic. Geographic separation has been a particularly difficult problem for traditional library access. But technology now provides solutions to assist librarians in getting information to their users. Users can dial-in to catalogs, indexes, and databases; they can transmit questions, reference problems, or document requests; and they can receive document delivery via fax. Technology demonstrates how good it can be when it is used to remove geographic barriers to information.

Technology and remote access information services remind librarians that if they can communicate with their users, they can teach. Information management education librarians can respond to remote users by designing computer assisted instruction programs, such as online tutorials and textbooks. By employing new tools like HyperCard and other hypertext programs within existing online catalogs, librarians provide innovative instruction and lessons to users at their point of need. Remote users also challenge librarians to design network interfaces and help systems that are appealing and motivating, as well as instructive.

In addition to some of the techniques mentioned above, the question of how information management education can respond to remote users challenges teaching librarians to collaborate with other faculty in finding the best means of using technology for instructional purposes. Teaching faculty face the same difficulty of communicating with remote student populations. By joining with faculty, librarians can formulate models that guide the development of programs ideally suited to long-distance teaching. Collaborating with faculty in research is another activity for information management education librarians. Asking how long-distance learning takes place and what is the best means of using technology for instruction are some of the many issues that still require investigation. Research projects that report on the advantages of using technology for teaching as well as how the disadvantages can be overcome are necessary to assist the library profession in fulfilling its teaching role.

Future Prospects

Professional associations like the Association of College and Research Libraries and its Bibliographic Instruction Section, the Medical Library Association, and the Association of Academic Health Sciences Library Directors play an important role in identifying trends within the profession, analyzing the trends for meaning and insight, and charting directions for the future development of its members. The trends seen in the health sciences arena indicate a changing user influenced by a growing and complex information environment utilizing new technologies to manage an information-dependent world. Given the conditions of a changing user, what are the future prospects for information management education services? Certainly, such prospects include continuously adapting to the user's needs with specific attention paid to expanding librarians' roles in educational services.

One important document that has helped health sciences librarians focus on the future is the Matheson-Cooper report, *Academic Information in the Academic Health Sciences Center: Roles for the Library in Information Management* (1982). While it is close to ten years since this report was issued, the ideas expressed by Matheson and Cooper are still valid, and they continue to inspire and guide health sciences librarians toward future roles much different from what currently occurs in most libraries. The central thrust of the report is to define a vision of the role of libraries, librarians, and information resources within academic health sciences centers. This vision derives from the effect libraries and librarians have on the nature of the work and activities that take place within academic health sciences centers. The problems associated with information management are viewed chiefly from the impact that technologies play in delivering information to the user. The report analyzes the current problem of information overload in light of both present and future applications of information technology. The future scenarios described by Matheson and Cooper ranged from five to twenty years, and in each scenario the report outlines the stages of change that occur with implementing technology: replacing old methods with more effective ones, doing current activities in new ways, and finally, changing behaviors as a result of new activities not yet realized. Many recommendations mentioned in the report are by now in place, such as integrated library systems and networking capabilities that link libraries to other libraries, to users, and to other outside institutions. Also, new ideas foreseen in the report are

about to be tested, such as developing the library as a knowledge management center.

The importance of the Matheson-Cooper report cannot
be underemphasized even at this date, since it remains instrumental in shaping the vision of health sciences librarians,
especially those responsible for education-related activities.
The report (1982, 36) re-emphasizes the two great themes of
medical education at the end of the twentieth century: that
learning is life-long and that what is learned is now less
important than how to learn.

> Education for the future requires learning how to
> learn. The goal today, as it was for Comenius in
> the 17th century, is to find a method of instruc-
> tion by which teachers teach less but learners
> learn more. But this does not mean more in a
> quantitative sense. We have passed the point of
> absurdity in a quantitative sense... The challenge
> is to learn in a more qualitative sense.

What roles did Matheson and Cooper (1982, 37) identify
for librarians to play in the education of health care practitioners?

> There are two aspects to the education issue.
> One is to learn problem-solving and decision
> process skills needed to use the facts and content
> base of medicine effectively. The other is to
> learn how to develop and manage a personal
> knowledge base that exploits the computer as a
> personal tool. It is to this latter effort that the
> library and the librarian can make a significant
> contribution.

Other roles include teaching students to manipulate a host of networks and databases from which information is drawn as well as to participate in the students' group learning process.

In a way, the Matheson-Cooper report, by stressing the importance of using information technologies to manage information, foretells another prospect for information management education librarians. Future roles will exist in the area of medical informatics. How to use the technology for information management will be important to faculty, staff, and students of all the health science schools. Users will not only demand friendly systems, but will look to the information professional to assist them in making sense of how and what they retrieve. Because of these user demands and because they already possess skills for managing information resources, librarians will have the opportunity to collaborate with other professionals engaged in informatics work through teaching principles of information management within health sciences curricula, participating in or conducting research projects measuring how information is created, shaped, disseminated, used and reused, or producing software for computer-assisted learning.

Involvement in medical informatics work will impact on the librarian's educational role. By demonstrating their skills in manipulating electronic information resources, librarians will be asked to teach those skills, and the principles they are based upon, to students and faculty alike. Because of its importance to research and patient care activities, instruction for information management will be decidedly integrated into the formal curriculum. Moore (1989, 26) comments that "The teaching role of the librarian has been discussed and debated, but the fact remains that more and more health sciences librarians are teaching in formal settings." The increasing volume of information facing professional practitioners along with the need to use the personal computer as a management tool and the realization that the professional curriculum must accommodate informatics concepts, will increase the trend to have librarians fully participate in the formal curriculum. Experience with library-based instruction service, such as programs on end-user searching, personal file management, and database design and construction, prepares information management education librarians for a more enhanced and developed role as teachers. Recognition of this teaching experience will increase and continue to influence how librarians are viewed within the academic medical center and especially within the individual academic program.

Still another prospect for the future work of information management education librarians is dealing with the quality issue. The ideal professional--regardless of discipline--strives to provide the highest quality of service possible. The problem facing librarians is to educate users, who are managing their own information, in how to define and evaluate information in a qualitative sense. The quality of information retrieval, for example, is not fully addressed by either user or librarian. Consider these difficult questions: How do users know that they have achieved a successful search of their topic's literature? and, How do users recognize a comprehensive search from a "quick and dirty" search? A related problem that faces all health care professionals is one of recognizing quality literature, i.e., separating the wheat from the chaff, the reliable from the useless. Who will teach students, for example, how to "read" the literature that they identified in their MEDLINE searches for content and understanding? Self-directed learning must not stop with the means of finding the information but must also continue to the final end: reading the information and determining that it is both valid and applicable to the immediate problem at hand.   Health science librarians have already encountered the quality issue at their end of the information cycle when they recognize the "satisfied but inept" user, as reported by Plutchak (1989, 45). This is the user who gets caught up in the process of searching databases for the thrill of it. These are users who show signs of entrenchment, unwilling to change behavior in order to learn better, more efficient, and more precise ways to search databases, or to realize that there are other sources to consider, or how to select the best litera-ture from the entire mass of information available to them. The quality of what users retrieve from the various information systems will become a major issue for librarians to address.

Conclusion

The three questions posed at the beginning of this chapter attempt to define the changing user in relation to information management education services. The context for exploring this relationship is the health sciences library. The relationship is characterized by a number of factors:

1) How well librarians know their users; the descriptive labels and assumptions about informa-tion needs will not suffice as a basis for establish-ing educational programs.
2) How users are affected by the forces of change within their respective information envi-ronments, namely, the impact of technology within that environment, the exponential growth of information, and the user's awareness and acceptance that learning is lifelong.
3) How effective librarians are at using technol-ogy to break down barriers between them and their users, and how librarians can use technology as a teaching tool.

The future of information management education
services appears promising for health sciences librarians for a
number of reasons. The health sciences professions are eager
to change their curricula and incorporate information management principles and techniques into programs of study. The
new field of medical informatics is likely to continue its growth
through research, innovation, and integration into the curriculum, and librarians will play significant educational roles within
that discipline. Outstanding issues, such as quality control in
information retrieval, also indicate a need for librarians as
teachers to address user problems in this area.

Librarians may prepare for working with the changing
user by sharing their experiences with each other and learning
from each other. Frequent sharing of ideas is necessary for
defining and advancing the library profession's education
agenda within higher education. Collaboration across library
cultures is important for achieving this end.

In many respects the nuances that separate health
sciences libraries from other academic libraries are just that--
subtle points that mark one library culture from another. The
differences are real and important for defining the unique
characteristics within the branches of librarianship but the
essence within each branch is still the same. What is said about
the future of information management education in health
sciences libraries could be said of bibliographic instruction in
academic libraries. The ultimate goal is that the user is served
through a timely and appropriate educational program. The
profession has a responsibility to users to provide a service
whereby they become information literate, mindful of the ways
information is acquired, organized, and managed, and how
information can be obtained to serve a particular need.

References

Association of American Medical Colleges. 1984. *Physicians for the Twenty-First Century,* the GPEP Report, Report of The Panel on the General Professional Education of the Physician and College Preparation for Medicine. Washington, D.C.: The Association.

Barnett, Octo. 1989. "Information technology and undergraduate medical education," *Academic Medicine* 64 (April): 187.

Blois, M.S. 1986. "What is medical informatics," *Western Journal of Medicine* 145: 776-777.

Burrow, G. N. 1990. "The body of medical knowledge required today far exceeds what students can learn in 4 years," *Chronicle of Higher Education* 36 (June 2): B1, B3.

Hackleman, Karen T. and Frances A. Bischoff. 1990. "Introduction: Symposium, The evolving role of the health sciences library in continuing education," *Bulletin of the Medical Library Association.* 78 (April): 155-156.

Hamilton, D. P. 1990. "Publishing by - and for? - The Numbers," *Science* 250 (December 7): 1331-1332.

Huth, Edward J. 1989. "The information explosion," *Bulletin of the New York Academy of Medicine.* 65 (July-August): 647-61.

Katz, William A. 1978. *Introduction to Reference Work.* Vol. 2, 3rd ed. New York: McGraw-Hill.

Kotzin, Sheldon and Kathi Eichenberger. 1990. "Use of MEDLARS Databases." Presented at the annual meeting of the Medical Library Association, Detroit, Michigan, May 21.

Matheson, Nina and John A. D. Cooper. 1982. "Academic information in the academic health sciences center: roles for the library in information management," *Journal of Medical Education.* 57 (October, pt. 2): 1-93.

McCool, Donna L. 1989. "Staffing for bibliographic instruction: issues and strategies for new and expanding programs." In: *Integrating library use skills into the general education curriculum*, edited by Maureen Pastine and Bill Katz. New York: Haworth Press.

Metz, Paul and Paul M. Gherman. 1991. "Serials pricing and the role of the electronic journal," *College & Research Libraries.* 52 (July): 413-327.

Moore, Mary. 1989. "Innovation and education: unlimited potential for the teaching library," *Bulletin of the Medical Library Association* 77 (January): 26-32.

National Library of Medicine. 1986. *Locating and gaining access to medical and scientific literature.* Long Range Plan, Report of Panel 2. Bethesda, MD: The Library.

Plutchak, T. Scott. 1989. "On the satisfied but inept end user," *Medical Reference Services Quarterly* 8 (Spring): 45-48.

Shedlock, James. 1983. "The library liaison program: building bridges with our users," *Medical Reference Services Quarterly* 2 (Spring): 61-65.

Shortliffe, Edward H. and Leslie E. Perreault, eds. 1990. *Medical Informatics, Computer Applications in Health Care*. Reading, MA: Addison-Wesley Publishing Company, 1990.

Wallingford, Karen T., Betsy L. Humphreys, Nancy E. Selinger, and Elliot R. Siegel. 1990. "Bibliographic retrieval: a survey of individual users of MEDLINE," *MD Computing* 7 (May-June): 166-71.

CURRICULUM REFORM: THE ROLE OF ACADEMIC LIBRARIES

Maureen Pastine
Linda Wilson

Educational Reform Movement

The educational reform movement of the 1980s produced a number of reports that criticized the quality of public schools and higher education in the United States. An example is a report by Ernest L. Boyer and the Carnegie Foundation for the Advancement of Teaching (1987, 5) entitled *College: The Undergraduate Experience in America*. The authors stated: "Increasingly, state and national education officials, lawmakers, parents, and students are wondering just how much is being learned." Most of these reports addressed curriculum reform, with a major theme revolving around the need for new learning and teaching models. In one of these, *The Paideia Proposal*, the respected educator Mortimer Adler (1982, 50) wrote, "All genuine learning is active, not passive. It involves the use of the mind, not just the memory. It is a process of discovery, in which the student is the main agent, not the teacher." The report on high schools by Boyer and the Carnegie Foundation (1983, 312) echoed this sentiment in its recommendation:

> Teachers should use a variety of teaching styles--
> lecturing to transmit information, coaching to
> teach a skill and Socratic questioning to enlarge

> understanding. But there should be particular
> emphasis on the active participation of the stu-
> dent.

The focus on active learning was later emphasized in the *Final Report of the American Library Association Presidential Committee on Information Literacy*, (1989, 22). To ensure a climate conducive to students becoming information literate, there must be a "move from textbook and lecture-style learning to resource-based learning." The report continued:

> Inherent in the concepts of information literacy
> and resource-based learning is the complementa-
> ry concept of the teacher as a facilitator of
> student learning rather than as presenter of
> ready-made information.

The focus of this chapter is to review the movements towards information literacy, curriculum reform, and the need for a more information-based or resource-centered teaching rather than the more traditional lecturing/reserve reading model. The authors describe the benefits to be derived from the complementary relationships that exist between the classroom and the library and between the teaching faculty and the librarian. The use of online networking and new technologies as means of building a closer liaison between librarians and teaching faculty is emphasized.

Information Literacy Movement

Recently there has been a movement in higher education to place greater emphasis on independent learning and continuing education. Paralleling this development is an increased focus on an individual's right to access information that can enhance his or her life. This information is needed to meet a wide range of recreational, personal, business, and educational needs. The *ALA Presidential Committee on Information Literacy* (1989, 22) report states:

> To be information literate, a person must be able to recognize when information is needed and have the ability to locate, evaluate, and use effectively the needed information. Ultimately information literate people are those who have learned how to learn. They know how knowledge is organized, how to find information, and how to use it in such a way that others can learn from them.

This commitment to new learning and teaching styles, which is a cornerstone of the information literacy movement, raises critical questions related to curriculum reform in higher education: Can higher education embrace the concept of information literacy? Has the information age caused faculty to radically change the content of their courses, based on the spreading realization that they cannot be expected to know everything on a particular subject? How much should faculty become involved in bibliographic instruction programs? How meaningful (or superficial) are current "integrated" curriculum initiatives, e.g., writing across the curriculum or developmental skills? There are no easy answers to these questions and each institution will have to respond based upon its own analysis. Achieving a better understanding of how faculty themselves perceive curriculum reform is at the center of such analyses. Is an understanding of the expectations of faculty in terms of outcomes of teaching especially important?

Faculty Response to Curriculum Reform

There is no doubt that university faculty are concerned both about students' acquisition of knowledge as well as their development of critical thinking and problem-solving skills. This concern is expressed in a number of reports and books, such as the National Commission on Excellence in Education's 1983 report, *A Nation at Risk: The Imperative for Education Reform*; the Carnegie Foundation's special report (1985) by Frank Newman entitled *Higher Education and the American*; and Alan Bloom's *The Closing of the American Mind*. But there has yet been no evidence of major changes in teaching methodologies towards a more independent or self-directed learning mode.

Although most faculty acknowledge the ideal of resource-based, self-directed learning, few professors seem successful in achieving it. Part of the reason can be traced to the public's criticism that students do not know "historical facts" upon graduation. Thus, faculty feel a responsibility to deliver such information to their students. They want to be sure that their students know the *content* of the subject--the basic concepts, theories, principles, historical figures, dates, and facts. As a result they have little time to teach the bibliographical literature of a field, how to identify, locate, access, retrieve, evaluate, and use it. In fact, many faculty members, not having the benefit themselves of a solid education in research methodology, are unaware of the library's resources, human and otherwise.

Because of this tendency toward a broader coverage of time and scope, there is an intensified focus on assigned readings and reserve materials. In addition, there is a greater reliance on lecturing and in-class discussion, resulting in less classroom time devoted to library use skills and research methodologies. Patricia H. Smith, et al., (n.d., 16), state that there should be more "hands-on learning and the discovery method as opposed to rote memorization and lectures." This mode of teaching, i.e., individualized learning, leads to more effective use of library resources.

The Value of Research Skills in Life-Long Learning

Unfortunately, however, much of the literature on curriculum reform from the educational establishment, as Patricia Senn Breivik (1989, 344) reported, "saw no role for librarians or libraries in issues related to quality education." This is ironic given the clear relationship between information access skills and the ability for one to keep up-to-date in one's field, to conduct research, to question, and to build on previously gained knowledge. After all, what is the benefit of subject content knowledge without these additional personal resources? It is commonly accepted knowledge that fewer than half of the nation's graduates work in their major field of specialization after attainment of a degree. It follows, then, that possessing information access skills is far more valuable than knowing facts that may be outdated or irrelevant to one's occupation. The research process enables people to develop the ability to formulate appropriate questions regarding problems, to develop the bibliographical abilities required to locate what others have discovered and concluded about the same problems, and to complete their own investigations.

Colleges and universities purport to teach life-long learning skills. To take this goal seriously requires much less reliance on lecturing and large group instruction, and more emphasis on individual learning or small group instruction where students learn on their own and from each other.

Similar guidance is provided by Lynne V. Cheney (1988, 5) in *Humanities in America*:

> Formal education should follow a plan of study aimed at comprehensive vision, not just of the present, but of the past. It should convey how the ideas and ideals of our civilization have evolved, thus providing a basis for understanding other cultures. It should provide a framework for lifelong learning about ourselves and the world in which we live.

Cheney goes on to discuss a letter from Professor Leon Kass (1988, 11) of the University of Chicago:

> Teaching is all too often filling empty vessels with information about, rather than initiating the young into thinking and feeling with, the books they read.

There is no single instructional method that is best for teaching everyone, but striving to enable students to make connections between what they already know in one field to the study of another subject field builds on previous knowledge and the development of conceptual learning skills. Making these connections allows students to place their existing knowledge within a broader context. In building connections it is crucial to learn how to locate and evaluate information to create new knowledge, and how to use it in one's own intellectual development and productivity. It is easy to forget subject content, dates, and facts taught. And what is accepted as truth today may be regarded as fallacy in future years based on further study and research. Thus, the ability to identify, locate, retrieve,

evaluate, and use information in the life-long quest for learning
becomes significant.

The Process of Education

The process of research is more important than the
product. Educators need to teach users how to think, not what
to think. Educational progress cannot be measured in terms of
mastery of specific information. The process of educating
should focus on the development of the critical thinking skills
and research strategies required to turn information into
knowledge. Students need to understand the processes and
systems for acquiring current and retrospective information, and
to be able to evaluate the effectiveness and reliability of those
information sources. A major part of the education process is
acquiring the skills necessary to choose and use information.
Interestingly enough, while many of the authors reporting on
the need for a more resource-based, self-directed type of
teaching/learning did not mention the critical importance of
libraries in the context of general education, they did point out
the necessity for using libraries effectively in gaining knowledge,
building upon it, and using it in one's own life-long learning
pursuits.
Others have noted the exclusion of libraries in these
reports, and they stress the importance of libraries to classroom
instruction. As Lynch and Seibert (1980, 136) report:

> The role of the librarian as faculty member has
> been determined by some to be critical to the
> implementation of a formal program of integrat-
> ing the library into the educational process.

From such reports a number of recommendations result, including that library instruction must be an integral part of classroom instruction, with students working as much in the library as in the classroom; that library funding must be substantial enough to provide students with the resources needed to supplement and enrich the texts and encourage further research and study; that students must be motivated not only by the printed word and classroom/library participation, but through special seminars, workshops, and media demonstrations that challenge the mind outside of the classroom through talks by authors, music and theatrical productions, film/video showings, and similar productions and discussions.

The failure to view library user education programs as integral to general education curriculum initiatives is criticized in an American Council of Education report by Suniewick and El-Khawas (1985, 7) that states:

> Over half the baccalaureate colleges but only 3 in 10 comprehensive and 2 in 10 doctorate universities required all undergraduates to have formal training in the use of the college library for research. This typically involved an orientation by library staff, rather than more intensive training conducted by faculty. Other forms of library training were cited by 20 percent of doctoral institutions and by 12 percent of other four-year institutions. These included self-tutorial programs undertaken through workbooks as well as specific courses on library research skills and work on library skills that was included as part of an English composition course or a literature course.

The Librarian's Role

In the face of these realities on college and university campuses, the academic librarian's overriding educational function is to promote and develop a library user education program that will exploit the complementary and implicit relationship between subject content and research skills for lifelong learning. Essential to this task are what Breivik and Gee (1989, 42) call "faculty development efforts"-- efforts on the part of academic librarians to accomplish the following:

> *   keeping faculty apprised of new information sources and services in their own field of research
> *   familiarizing faculty with relevant resources and services beyond their areas of specialization
> *   familiarizing faculty and/or their assistants and secretaries with the time-saving tools and services of the library
> *   helping faculty understand the research capabilities and needs of their students
> *   working with faculty in structuring experiences that will effectively promote the mastery of information-management skills.

The need for librarians to make their services and expertise more visible is underscored by Wiberly and Jones (1989, 638) who point out:

> From earlier studies of scholarly information seeking, principally surveys, we had learned that scholars rely, first, on the references in publications they read; second, on communications from

colleagues; third, on formal bibliography; and fourth, on librarians.

For library user education to be viewed as being vital to the curriculum, librarians must take an active role in educating faculty about its value. In this regard it is crucial for librarians to have a voice in the educational process by seeking involvement in policy-making educational committees, curriculum committees, and review boards on the campus. Patricia Battin (1984, 174-5) notes the importance of librarians gaining seats on university policy councils and suggests the following six policy areas to target:

1) Centralized long-range planning and budgetary planning groups on campus;
2) Integrated information services with academic programs and priorities;
3) Access to scholarly resources;
4) Development of electronic publications on campus;
5) Copyright and ownership issues;
6) Research and development in information technology.

The opportunities for librarians and teaching faculty to work together as equal partners in the educational process are many. The information resources and online catalogs of many hundreds of libraries now accessible on the Internet provide an excellent way for the librarian to introduce the faculty to new methods to access information and to use online resources within and outside of the classroom in their teaching methodologies. In this "teaching library" environment, a concept beginning with the "library college" concept and one promoted by Hannelore Rader (1986), is that librarians are seen as "experts in organizing information and in teaching users how to access and evaluate information in different formats." The teaching library model continues to gain support as rapid developments in technology force faculty and administration into closer collaboration with those knowledgeable in accessing the explosion of information available electronically.

New Opportunities For Librarians

On many academic campuses today there is a movement toward changes in organizational titles and reporting structures in universities where, for example, the number of library directors being appointed to such positions as Vice Provost for Information, Director of Information Resources, and Chair of Telecommunications Policy Groups is increasing. These changes are placing libraries and computer centers in an even more strategic position than in past years. Because of the new technologies, faculty, researchers, students, and librarians are faced with a myriad of new ways, primarily electronic, to gain information and to expand the environment from which one obtains information resources for routine work, study, and research. Both libraries and computer centers and their personnel have the opportunity to use this strategic position to demonstrate the power of bibliographic and nonbibliographic databases. It provides valuable opportunities to ally more closely and to integrate all segments of the university into more collaborative roles where cross-disciplinary and interdisciplinary boundaries are expanded and enriched. The librarian's role is to ensure that faculty understand that they and their students are no longer limited to resources held locally, that they may use technologies within the classroom to build educational connections and links to world-wide experts and authorities and to databanks far beyond the limitations of the home library. Most important of all, the librarian can demonstrate that the new technologies provide incredible linkages to bridge the gap between what is taught in the classroom and what is available in the library--i.e., the library can become the classroom or vice versa.

Changing Demands On the Librarian's Time

Unfortunately, adding new goals to the librarian's workload occurs at a time when time, energy, and money are at a premium. The renewed educational focus, new technologies, and enhanced networking capabilities have expanded the librarian's role. At the same time, less time is available in which to address large numbers of students in classes--even though the actual numbers of classes taught have increased. In some cases, the demands made by students in lower level general education courses--e.g., English Composition, Elementary/Secondary Education, Speech Communications, World Civilization, and the Human Environment--mean less time to devote to upper division and graduate level students.

The new technologies and online systems, remote access capabilities, and greater resource sharing and networking have changed librarians' approaches to meeting the demands of users. Online instruction is no longer limited to the reference librarian acting as intermediary for online commercial databases. Increasingly, other library personnel are active participants in library user education, both to library clientele and to the library staff. Few, if any, academic libraries have not had to make radical changes in operations and services in order to attempt to meet increased user demands, most requiring additional and new methods of instruction for both staff and user. New services require increased financial commitments under increasingly tight fiscal constraints.

The in-house training, re-education, and professional development needed to meet an expanded campus-wide educational role have had a dramatic impact on the role of librarians. Libraries' organizational structures are changing, as are the expectations for, and the expertise required of, all levels of staff. The result is increased stress and sometimes even deterioration of morale as librarians realize they must gain new expertise, new knowledge, new debts, and increased demands on their time, as well as, more importantly, new challenges to renew and invigorate them. Are libraries responding in appropriate ways? Can the new and changing needs and demands be met without bankrupting libraries and overwhelming staff and students?

The Future Education Role of Libraries

There has been a proliferation of articles, conferences, and papers addressing the question of whether or not the library will remain a viable, dynamic force in information dissemination and retrieval once library users become computer literate end users of the many developing systems and networks. All indications are that the library will not diminish as a force in acquiring, accessing, and retrieving knowledge, nor in educating the library user. In fact, just the reverse may be true.

At a number of institutions, innovative programs have been instituted to ensure the central role of the library in the scholarly process. In most academic libraries the gate count has remained steady, but the circulation, interlibrary loan, reference, user education, and systems services have increased dramatically, along with liaison relationships to extended university services, telecommunications, and computing center personnel, instructional technology/media services, and other campus offices.

A number of libraries have already revamped programs and services to place increased emphasis on teaching roles related to using the new technologies. Staff at Cornell's Albert R. Mann Library have targeted students in their Biological Sciences and Business/Finance disciplines to participate in a specially developed information literacy curriculum, spanning a time period of several years. With the help of grant money, librarians are evaluating the program using pre- and post-tests with students and surveying employers for their perception of what information literacy skills are needed by students after graduation. In another example of how academic libraries can play a primary role in educating for the information age, librarians at Virginia Polytechnic Institute and State University have developed a graduate course entitled "Information Technology" that is taught as part of the sequence of courses necessary for a doctoral degree in the College of Education's instructional technology program. And according to the *Library Journal* (1990, 44):

> The University of Southern California has received a $1 million grant from the Fletcher Jones Foundation for the construction of a teaching library. The library, which will be built on the University Park campus, will be home to the Fletcher Jones Foundation New Technology Demonstration and Evaluation Center. The library will have a core collection of 120,000 volumes as well as 'hundreds' of individual computer and audiovisual workstations. The New Technology Demonstration and Evaluation Center will be used for demonstrating software

being considered for inclusion in teaching programs. The library is...scheduled to open in the
spring of 1993.

The Changing Demands of Library Users

The most time-consuming workload, interestingly
enough, has been the increase in user education related to the
revamping of general education curricula and teaching students
and faculty uses of information via new technologies. Some
teaching faculty and some library staff may be slow to adapt to
the newer technologies and expanded access capabilities, but
students are not. Their demands increase daily as they use
electronic sources and other new technologies. They want
retrospective conversion completed immediately so they do not
have to use the card catalog. They want more public access
terminals. They want microcomputer labs in the libraries.
They want to be able to download, upload, merge, and print
data from a variety of sources, easily and with little or no
training. They do not want to know they are using different
systems or different databases. They do not want to know that
by relying so extensively on automation and new technologies,
they may be missing some important retrospective data or data
not available in machine-readable form.

New problems are arising in teaching students to conduct
research in a comprehensive manner and to know the adequa-
cies and inadequacies of bibliographic control in a discipline, as
well as the limitations of what is and is not available in
electronic format. The challenge presented to academic
libraries by these issues will continue and cannot be resolved
quickly. University libraries and many other educational
institutions are making strides in increasing visibility, improving

the public image of librarians as knowledgeable experts, and building closer liaisons to their constituencies.

The convergence of curriculum reform with new technologies presents other challenges as well, not the least of which is the cost issue. Resource-based learning in all disciplines increasingly depends on computerized resources. Every library must make decisions not only about which databases to buy, and in what format, but also about who will pay the cost. When fee-based services are provided, the potential exists for a polarization of information-rich and information-poor classes of users. Libraries must ask, and attempt to answer, difficult questions, such as: What level of access to information, if any, is provided without cost to users? If fees are to be charged for specified levels of access, what is the most equitable fee structure that can be instituted?

Conclusion

Even though librarians are feeling the stress imposed by reduced funding, inadequate staffing to meet needed traditional as well as new demands, and technology-related issues, they are also beginning in many academic libraries nationwide to focus on planning new directions for educational roles. Their expanded roles at universities are in direct accord with the underlying goals of curriculum reform. Librarians are in a unique position to be true advocates for resource-based learning in all disciplines. Because they are less territorial, they are able to focus on broader educational needs than faculty members who have strong allegiance to specific fields of study.

In order to exploit fully their new role in the "teaching library," librarians will need to break out of the traditional reactive mode to become leaders, initiators, creators, designers, and facilitators. Teaching faculty are beginning to see librarians

in a new light and to rely on them, both to assist in planning
curricular reform and to assume a greater educational role in
teaching students how to conduct research in increasingly
sophisticated ways. The answers may not be clear, but by
providing leadership in new modes of teaching and learning,
librarians will ensure their value and viability in the current
wave of curriculum reform and in subsequent reform movements.

References

Adler, Mortimer. 1982. *The Paideia Proposal: An Educational
    Manifesto*. New York: Macmillan Publishing Co.

*American Library Association Presidential Committee on Infor-
    mation Literacy*. 1989.   Chicago: American Library
    Association.

Battin, Patricia. 1984. "The Library: Center of the Restructured
    University," *College & Research Libraries*. 45 (May):
    170-176.

Bloom, Alan. 1987. *The Closing of the American Mind: How
    Higher Education Has Failed Democracy and Impover-
    ished the Souls of Today's Students*. New York: Simon
    and Schuster.

Boyer, Ernest L. 1987. The Carnegie Foundation for the
    Advancement of Teaching. *College: The Undergraduate
    Experience in America*. New York: Harper & Row.

Boyer, Ernest L. 1983. The Carnegie Foundation for the
    Advancement of Teaching. *High School: A Report on*

Secondary Education in America. New York: Harper & Row.

Breivik, Patricia Senn. 1989. "Politics for Closing the Gap," in *Integrating Library Use Skills into the General Education Curriculum,* edited by Maureen Pastine and Bill Katz. New York: Haworth.

Breivik, Patricia Senn and E. Gordon Gee. 1989. *Information Literacy: Revolution in the Library.* New York: American Council of Education and Macmillan.

Cheney, Lynne V. 1988. *Humanities in America: A Report to the President, the Congress, and the American People.* Washington D.C.: National Endowment for the Humanities.

Lynch, Beverly P. and Karen S. Seibert. 1980. "The Involvement of the Librarian in the Total Educational Process," *Library Trends.* 29 (Summer): 127-138.

National Commission on Excellence in Education. 1983. *A Nation at Risk: The Imperative for Education Reform.* Washington D.C.: National Commission on Excellence in Education.

Newman, Frank. 1985. *Higher Education and the American Resurgence.* Carnegie Foundation. Princeton, New Jersey: Princeton University Press.

Rader, Hannelore B. 1986. "The Teaching Library Enters the Electronic Age," *College & Research Libraries News.* 47 (June): 402-404.

Smith, Patricia H., et al. n.d. *Illiteracy in America: Extent, Causes, and Suggested Solutions*. The National Advisory Council on Adult Education Literacy Committee. Washington D.C.: U.S. Government Printing Office.

Suniewick, Nancy and Elaine El-Khawas. 1985. *General Education Requirements in the Humanities*. Washington D.C.: American Council on Education, Higher Education Panel Reports, Number 66 (October): 25.

Tompkins, Philip. 1990. "New Structures for Teaching Libraries," *Library Administration & Management.* 4 (Spring): 77-81.

"USC gets $1 Million Grant for Teaching Library." 1990. *Library Journal.* 115 (December): 44.

Wiberly, Jr., Stephen E. and William G. Jones. 1989. "Patterns of Information Seeking in the Humanities," *College & Research Libraries.* 50 (November): 638-645.

INFORMATION LITERACY: ONE RESPONSE TO THE NEW DECADE

Hannelore Rader
William Coons

Academic librarians in the 1990s, because of their expertise in organizing and accessing information, are uniquely positioned to make a vital contribution to higher education. This contribution occurs most profitably when academic leaders at the campus and national level view librarians as natural and active partners in the educational process. By exploring ways in which librarians can align their goals and objectives with the educational mission of the institution, academic leaders can create a synergistic environment where the library's resources and its educational programs work together to develop students who are self-directed, independent, lifelong learners, and consumers of information.

Several reports were written during the last decade that called for colleges and universities to encourage the development of curricula which emphasize "active learning" strategies. In *College: the Undergraduate Experience in America*, Ernest Boyer (1987) reports the findings of the Carnegie Foundation for the Advancement of Teaching. The book provides a study of the American undergraduate experience and how it affects the lives of students. It identifies various tension points that must be examined to improve college education in the United States. The report ends with "a guide to a good college" that incorporates a higher priority for independent study using the college library. The college library should be looked upon as an important piece of the undergraduate experience and the library staff should be considered partners in the teaching process. The students should receive bibliographic instruction and be taught to view the library as a central learning resource. Librarians must be able to understand undergraduate education and work closely with classroom teachers to enrich the undergraduate experience.

Time for Results, The Governors' 1991 Report on Education, (1986) examines how higher education outcomes are measured. It makes the point that the quality of a college education can no longer be measured by counting books in the library or laboratory equipment. Instead, post secondary education must be measured by student learning and performance.

Complementing these reports are documents issued by various library organizations, such as the American Association of School Librarians and the Association for Education Communications and Technology, and the American Library Association Presidential Committee on Information Literacy. These documents focus on the library's contribution to the "active learning" process in terms of "information literacy." Although these documents vary in their emphasis, they agree that an information literate person is able to (1) understand the process of acquiring current and retrospective information and manipulate systems and services that locate and retrieve that information, (2) evaluate the effectiveness and reliability of various information channels and sources, including libraries, for various kinds of needs, (3) master specific basic skills in acquiring and storing information (e.g., facility in using databases, spreadsheets, and word processing packages, as well as books, journals, and report literature), (4) recognize and articulate current and future public policy issues relating to information. These documents maintain that information literacy is an integral part of undergraduate education, analogous to the "writing across the curriculum" initiative that recognizes writing as an integrative skill that can be developed at any point in the educational process.

This paper explains how this approach can be applied to an information literacy program by answering these questions:

> 1) What concepts and skills define an "information literate" person?
> 2) How should bibliographic instruction programs respond to the challenge of information literacy?
> 3) How does the evolution of the "electronic university" affect the role of the bibliographic instruction?

Libraries can be more active partners in educational arenas both at the campus and the national levels. They have unique contributions to make toward accomplishing institutional goals. These contributions include but are not limited to the following: (1) libraries provide a meaningful framework for the knowledge and information needed in all disciplines; (2) libraries constitute an ideal environment for problem-solving within their vast information storage; (3) students can obtain problem-solving and information-handling skills from librarians; (4) libraries provide a natural environment for life-long learning. Libraries can contribute to the educational mission of the academic institution by becoming more fully integrated into the academic curriculum. This will encourage a much needed focus on student learning in order to prepare them for complex problem solving in a global setting. These contributions by librarians are possible in institutions with strong academic leadership that breaks old stereotypes and molds, and devises means to fully and effectively use library resources.

Academic libraries can contribute to higher education by aligning their goals and objectives with the educational mission of the institution. Reports on higher education identify the need for more active learning whereby students become self-directed, independent learners who are prepared for life-long learning. To accomplish this, students need to understand: the processes and systems for acquiring current and retrospective information; how to manipulate systems and services for locating and receiving information; how to evaluate the effectiveness and reliability of various information channels and sources, including libraries, for various kinds of needs; how to master certain basic skills in acquiring and storing their own information, e.g. skills with databases, spreadsheets, word and information processing, and skills with books, journals, and report literature; and how to recognize and articulate current and future public policy issues relating to information, e.g., copyright, privacy, and privatization of government information.

In order to make all this possible, information gathering and evaluation skills need to be mastered at the undergraduate as well as the graduate level, and learning opportunities should be integrated within existing departments, analogous to "writing across the curriculum", rather than stand-alone bibliographic instruction programs. Administrators, faculty and librarians should be engaged in creative new partnerships that transmit the life-long value and reward of the research to students. Information literacy should be a demonstrable outcome of higher education.

What Concepts and Skills Define an
"Information Literate" Person?

Information literacy may be defined as the ability to effectively access and evaluate information for problem solving and decision making. Information literate persons know how knowledge and information are organized, how to find various types of information, how to organize information, and how to use information in problem solving. To be information literate means to: be educated for survival and success in an information/technology environment; lead productive, healthy and satisfying lives in a democratic society; deal effectively with rapidly changing environments; solve the challenging problems of the 1990s in order to ensure a better future for the next generation; be an effective information consumer who can find appropriate information for personal and professional problem solving; have writing and computer proficiency; and to possess an integrated set of research strategy and education skills, and knowledge of discipline related tools and resources. In short, information literate people know how to be life-long learners in an information society.

How Should Bibliographic Instruction
Programs Respond to the Challenge
of Information Literacy?

To effect an information literacy program, bibliographic instruction programs can become an even more pervasive instruction component on campus. Librarians can intensify their work with teaching faculty in planning and implementing curricula that teach students information literacy concepts. This will be accomplished as more librarians become leaders within their academic communities and the rest of the campus looks to the library for management solutions to the burgeoning electronic information environment. The concept of information literacy can be woven into appropriate learning and teaching activities, and librarians can become trail-blazers in developing information literacy opportunities for all citizens. Librarians possess the experience with broad-scale educational programs, the dedication to public service, and commitment to the freedom of information: who better than they can marshal the resources to meet the information literacy challenge?

Some strategies to explore include assessing and explaining information technology's impact on higher education; working with complementary telecommunication and computer faculty to incorporate new information technologies into the curricula; teaching the management of information resources; educating the campus on the important role librarians can assume in ensuring information literacy for students (outreach); broadening the bibliographic instruction program to include the structure of information, new electronic formats, critical analysis of information, and the use of information to solve problems; and changing the name, content and identity of bibliographic instruction programs toward a broader concept. Labels such as information management and analysis, user education, or information literacy, while not ideal, convey a greater sense of the overall intent of librarians' instructional efforts than does the term "bibliographic instruction." As such they are more apt to make more sense to a non-librarian audience of deans, program directors, and presidents--individuals who often do not understand the educational possibilities of libraries--and influence both their thinking and their decision-making.

How Does the Evolution of the "Electronic University" Affect the Role of the Bibliographic Instruction Librarian?

America's colleges and universities are incorporating new technologies within instruction and research. Students are becoming more sophisticated in their understanding of an access to "the wired environment"; national networks such as NSFNet link remote resources and users; the scholars workstation is approaching reality; and partnerships, either administrative or collaborative, are occurring between libraries and computer centers. Universities are putting in place the groundwork (wiring/cabling) for powerful networks to enable them to utilize telecommunication for global learning and research.

The campus networks are making it possible to use classrooms as laboratories for active learning experiences for students. Information can be brought to the classroom, dormitory, office, and home from any type of source (global databases, television, videos, laboratories), using sophisticated telecommunication devices. New information infrastructures will be created for the electronic university.

As the "electronic university" evolves, the role of the library will also change. Electronic information technologies are bringing about major changes in academic libraries by making it mandatory for libraries to set up sophisticated telecommunication networks in cooperation with computing services. Changes will continue to impact libraries as they alter the way they collect and deliver information to their campus community. As new modes of storage and dissemination of information become available and artificial intelligence facilitates more user-friendly and human-machine interfaces, the character of the library will be radically altered. Libraries are on their way to becoming networks for accessing scholarly information and disseminating it electronically to their users. The need for training and education of users will grow extensively and librarians will find themselves increasingly in the role of "information educators" on campus. In the future, librarians must not only work for greater access to the information base of society, but must educate citizens to be able to use that information effectively and efficiently. The bibliographic instruction librarian is on the front line of the information profession and is responsible for understanding and using the various electronic media which constitute a growing percentage of the information base. OPAC's, CD's, and locally mounted data files are but a few of the resources which are introducing a new set of concepts and skills which need to be taught. The proliferation (and lack of standardization) of these resources are adding an amazing mix of complex technological requirements to the work of librarians.

Users are becoming more sophisticated and will expect librarians to know more too--more about database structure, more about software packages such as ProCite and Reference Manager, more about remote access. Bibliographic instruction librarians will be called upon to explain the maze of electronic resources, teach the criteria for selecting applications software, and introduce students to the components of the information production and distribution cycle.

Librarians' roles will become, without question, more expansive and complex, and appropriately so. Librarians will step out of the library and into the classroom and will complement instruction of library-based print resources to include alternative formats that are housed elsewhere. To retain their professional credibility, what librarians do and teach must reflect the evolving reality of the Information Age. Librarians will teach, but also advise, consult, and lead.

Bibliographic instruction librarians will have to be active learners who use and apply the resources they teach. They will need a rudimentary understanding of the operating systems and technical requirements of various resources (you never had to plug in and boot up a book) and a working familiarity with multiple formats. A positive attitude is important, as is the need to stop reacting to the technology that drives us and become responsible for and involved in the production, processing, and distribution of information (for example, contributing to interface design and database construction standards).

If librarians hope to keep pace with the developments in technology, assure the value of their contributions to education, and retain their roles as innovative organizers and disseminators of information, they must keep pace with changes in our society and with technology.

How Does Information Literacy Relate to Bibliographic Instruction?

When the automobile was first introduced, people did not know what to call it. Initially, it was defined on the basis of the past and acquired the name "horseless carriage". In a similar fashion, user education over the years has expanded and evolved in concept and scope from library orientation to library instruction, and from library instruction to bibliographic instruction. Each change that we have seen in the instruction jargon within libraries has progressed to the next higher plane, incorporating the concepts and issues of previous terminology. Bibliographic instruction is an example of this evolution. Twenty years ago it was recognized as more like library instruction than not. Would anyone today suggest that biblio-graphic instruction is simply library instruction with a new name? Of course not. While bibliographic instruction programs are gradually evolving from library instruction to incorporate database searching concepts, some evaluation of information sources, and the information production/distribution/consumption life cycle, the term bibliographic instruction is still overwhelmingly synonymous with short-range, library centered, print-bound instruction.

Is information literacy a unique, innovative concept, or simply bibliographic instruction with a new name? Information literacy is not a synonym for bibliographic instruction. It is an expansion of traditional materials and methods of user education. Information literacy adds another dimension by representing a broader approach and offering the opportunity to produce students who understand the importance of information, and who have the competence to locate, evaluate and manage it. Information literacy contributes towards a higher level of literacy. Bibliographic instruction is more often a situation-specific response, whereas information literacy contributes towards life-long learning by educating individuals to effectively utilize and evaluate information.

Distinct from bibliographic instruction both conceptually and pedagogically, information literacy serves to synthesize the pieces of the information puzzle into an integrated whole. *Information literacy has at its base the new communications and information technologies that are transforming society.* It is not just information finding but also understanding and evaluating, and there is a strong dependence on influencing attitudes and heightening awareness. Information literacy differs from bibliographic instruction in content and format (it is not bound to any media); in technique (the emphasis is on learning which is cumulative within a sequence of classes over time); in focus (not bound to what is within the walls of a library); and emphasis (it incorporates the invisible college, the research and publication process, and the range of issues relating to the production, distribution, access, evaluation and management of information).

The evolution in our society and our economy necessitates a shift in not only in *how* people are taught, but in *what* they are taught. Information literacy is a concept that students, faculty, and administrators identify with. They sense and appreciate its purpose, and support efforts to infuse it into the curriculum. As a term describing a process, it also allows librarians to break away from the misconceived library stereotypes and instruct with equal footing on new ground. Another way to approach information literacy is to see it as the goal, outcome, or product, and bibliographic instruction as one available method to achieve that goal.

Future Issues

During the course of the Think Tank the participants raised several questions concerning the concept of information literacy. They did not provide answers. They discussed and identified possibilities, but hope practicing librarians will provide suggestions and innovations to resolve these issues.

How can an information literate population be achieved when many libraries have yet to recognize their vital educational role and establish dynamic and effective instruction programs?

Librarianship and bibliographic instruction have come a long way in the last twenty years. The leaders of the movement may be proud of their achievements and contributions--but stop for a moment and look around: are there really that many institutions that believe in their mission enough to offer substantially funded, well staffed, carefully planned, and clearly articulated instruction programs? How many librarians continue to react to each situation as it arises, to teach the minimum, and subside until the next request? Librarians can no longer question their educational purpose--they do have a role to play in teaching users. Librarians must go beyond their present efforts and attempt to form additional teaching partnerships with faculty, allocate additional monies and staff, and develop innovative and dynamic means of communicating the attitudes, awareness, skills and knowledge that all students need.

Is information literacy a program for the privileged few, or an opportunity to empower the masses with the intellectual means to contribute to society and lead more productive lives?

It is important to be aware that the new developments in electronic information are not universally available. There are constituents, external to the academic environment, without understanding of or access to information. Librarians need to carefully examine their roles, as gatekeepers and educators, and partnerships to avoid excluding users. As computing and telecommunications technologies grow to dominate the information scene, challenges for instruction librarians will be to maintain an open portal for everyone's access, regardless of economic status or social status.

How can information literacy programs and academic libraries contribute to the economic development in the United States, especially in urban areas?

Librarians can form partnerships with the business community, social agencies, and public schools to ensure better education for the population, to ensure more productivity in industry, and to encourage innovations. Librarians can be instrumental in helping business people become information literate through appropriate professional programs on campus. Again, partnerships with faculty must be built to incorporate information literacy training in the business curriculum. Libraries can also offer the corporate world access to library resources through specialized fee-based services using appropriately trained librarians. Partnerships between businesses and libraries can, if prepared carefully, enhance fund-raising efforts on campus and achieve great visibility for the academic institution in the community, especially the urban community.

Who shall speak for information literacy, and what common goals and objectives will form the standards for measurement?

In addition to the ACRL/BIS Model Statement of Objectives for Academic Bibliographic Instruction and Learning Goals and Objectives supported by the ALA Presidential Committee on Information Literacy, there are numerous other documents from the public and school library community that could contribute to universal objectives, such as *Information Power* issued by American Association of School Librarians and the Association for Educational Communications and Technology in 1988. Even though there is no one who speaks for information literacy in a formal, representative fashion, the American Library Association has began an initiative in that direction by establishing the National Forum on Information Literacy, chaired by Patricia Breivik. In her 1990/91 progress report to the ALA Council, Breivik notes that "the Forum is committed to the integration of the concepts of information and resource-based learning into the policies and operations of its member organizations." She describes several major accomplishments regarding the integration of information literacy into curricula as promoted by the Association for Supervision and Curriculum Development, and the Middle States Association of Colleges and Schools Commission on Higher Education. The American Association of Higher Education has established an Action Committee on Information Literacy to address the topic at each annual conference. Future plans for the Forum include targeting twenty-five additional organizations for membership. However, common goals and objectives for measuring information literacy programs' outcome and for assessing an individual's information literacy level need to be developed.

How will information literacy affect the instruction librarian? What concepts and skills define the person imparting information literacy?

In all likelihood, the skills, talents, and prerequisites for being an instruction librarian will become more extensive. Every librarian will have to know more and learn more. Users will ask for assistance in selecting bibliographic file management software. Users will ask for assistance in extracting, interpreting, and processing data from numeric files. Users will ask to be led through the maze of electronic products and services, and offer recommendations. Expectations will increase, as will standards and stress levels. Schools of professional studies will need to meet these challenges, offer classes, and produce qualified teachers. Much depends upon effective and dynamic leadership from all levels of the profession-- instruction practitioners, library directors, and graduate school professors. Librarians will be challenged in the next decade, and it will be difficult for them to achieve all that they need and want. While librarians must ponder the future, they must also act to create it. Society needs teachers and transmitters of the skills and knowledge associated with information retrieval, access, and management.

Conclusion

It is obvious from the content of this paper that there are many more questions than answers regarding information literacy and that the issues surrounding this concept will provide the library profession with tremendous challenges in the last decade of the 20th Century. These challenges include:

1) development of intensive continuing education programs for bibliographic instruction librarians to prepare them for the broader role of helping students become information literate;

2) need for librarians to become more assertive and political regarding their role in developing and changing the curriculum to reflect information literacy training for students;

3) development of a unit within the organization that deals responsively with information literacy;

4) establishment of demonstration projects and sites for information literacy programs in higher education as well as cooperative information literacy between universities and schools;

5) development of standardized evaluation criteria to measure the outcomes of information literacy programs and to assess an individual's information literacy level.

In the future, bibliographic instruction librarians must become involved in addressing instructional issues on campus, not just in the library. The library profession must creatively address the training and development of new professionals to prepare them for the expanding educational roles of librarians on campus, and innovative leadership within the profession must be rewarded to handle the many challenges created by information literacy concerns and to identify librarians who can become change agents.

References

American Association of School Librarians and the Association for Educational Communications and Technology. 1988. *Information Power: Guidelines for School Library Media Programs*. Chicago: ALA.

American Library Association. Presidential Committee on Information Literacy. 1989. *Final Report*. Chicago: ALA. January.

American Library Association. Presidential Committee on Information Literacy. 1989. *Information Literacy: Background, Learning Goals, and Objectives*. Chicago: ALA. January.

Arms, Caroline. 1990. *Campus Strategies for Libraries and Electronic Information*. Rockport, MA: Digital Press.

Blake, Virgil L.P. and Renee Tjoumas, editors. 1990. *Information Literacies for the Twenty-First Century*. Boston: G.K. Hall, Inc.

Boyer, Ernest L. 1987. *College. The Undergraduate Experience in America*. New York: Harper & Row.

Breivik, Patricia S. and E. Gordon Gee. 1989. *Information Literacies for the Twenty-First Century.* New York: MacMillan.

Breivik, Patricia S. (1985). "A vision in the making: Putting libraries back in the information society." *American Libraries* 16 (November): 723.

Compaine, Benjamin M. 1984. *Information Technology and Cultural Change: Toward a New Literacy?* Cambridge: Harvard University's Center for Information Policy Research. September.

Demo, William. 1986. *The Idea of "Information Literacy" in the Age of High-Tech.* Washington, D.C.: EDRS. 1986 (ED 282 537).

Goodman, Kenneth S. 1985. "Commentary: On being literate in an age of information." *Journal of Reading.* 28 (February): 388-392.

Hamelink, Cees. 1976. "An alternative to news: A new 'information literacy' is necessary." *Journal of Communication.* 26 (Autumn): 120-124.

Horton, Forest Woody, Jr. 1983. "Information literacy vs. computer literacy." *ASIS Bulletin.* (April): 14-16.

Kuhlthau, Carol Collier, "Information skills for an information society: A review of research." *ERIC Digest*, (December).

Mensching, Glenn E., Jr. and Teresa B. Mensching. 1989. *Coping With Information Illiteracy: Bibliographic Instruction for the Information Age: Papers presented at the 17th National LOEX Library Instruction Conference held in Ann Arbor, Michigan. May 4-5.* Ann Arbor, Michigan: Pierian Press.

Michaels, Carolyn. 1985. *Library Literacy Means Lifelong Learning.* Metuchen, NJ: Scarecrow Press.

Moran, Barbara. 1989. "Academic libraries: Meeting the challenges of the electronic university." *Library Times International.* 6 (July): 1-2.

Nelson, Nancy. 1990. "Electronic Libraries: Vision and Implementation." *Computers in Libraries.* 10 (February): 6-13.

Nickerson, Raymond S. 1985. "Adult literacy and technology." *Visual Language.* XIX (Summer): 311-349.

Olsen, Jan Kennedy and Bill Coons. 1989. "Cornell University's information literacy program." In *Coping With Information Illiteracy: Bibliographic Instruction for the Information Age.* Ann Arbor, Michigan: Pierian Press.

Quinn, James, Joseph Kirkman, and Cora Jo Schultz. 1983. "Beyond Computer Literacy." *Educational Leadership* 41 (September) : 38-39,67.

Shill, Harold B. 1987. "Bibliographic instruction: Planning for electronic information environment." *College & Research Libraries* 48 (September): 433-453.

Taylor, Robert S. 1986. "Information literacy." In *Value-added Processes in Information Systems*. Norwood, NJ: Ablex Publishing Corporation.

Time for Results: The Governors' 1991 Report on Education. 1986. Washington, D.C.: National Governors' Association Center for Policy Research and Analysis.

EDUCATION FOR THE SECOND GENERATION OF BIBLIOGRAPHIC INSTRUCTION LIBRARIANS

Martha L. Hale

Education for the next generation of librarians must be considered in the context of the shifting paradigm, technology, and the image of the profession. This chapter will explore library education by examining the influence of people and experience on potential changes. Four specific examples of change in library/information science education are proposed in order to educate a generation of librarians who consider information literacy a primary responsibility.

Paradigm, Technology, and Image

According to Thomas Kuhn (1970) research in academic disciplines is conducted within the parameters of a paradigm until the puzzles being investigated outdistance the boundaries of the dominant paradigm. Because of the interaction among research, teaching, and practice, a paradigm affects all three as a lens affects vision. For example, when practice in the information professions focuses on local ownership, size of collection, and locating the book, the staff will concentrate on the materials. The courses in professional and continuing education will focus on collection development, sources, and classification. The research will address problems of catalog consistency, purchasing power, and identification of the best materials. The paradigm of a discipline in which one is educated influences what its philosophers can envision and what its practitioners value as legitimate activity. The paradigm influences what the researchers choose to study and how they interpret the results. The professors' plans for what should be taught to the next generation of practitioners are often influenced by the paradigm in which they themselves were educated.

When the activities of practice no longer serve a society, shifts in the activities of the practitioners often anticipate changes in research and teaching. Recent demands of users for access to the content within the resources, their requests for information to be reconfigured and repackaged into usable formats, the proliferation of numbers and media of information sources, and the availability of technologies that allow distant access require that practitioners, educators, and researchers address new issues. The old lens does not allow the insights needed for solving the new problems. The emerging paradigm appears to be more hospitable to the concepts of information literacy.

Volumes have been written on the influence of technology on library/information service and on library education. Certainly the curricula of Library/Information Science programs must shift to recognize the changing capabilities for access that technology encourages to include visual technologies and emerging multimedia technologies. Just as the typewriter allowed us to decide to eliminate library penmanship from the course of study, so now we must realize real-time processing, hypermedia stacks, electronic bulletin boards, and virtual reality are affecting the very nature of librarianship.

One reason change often seems to be instigated by people with little library experience or people educated outside of Master of Library Science programs is that these people bring alternative paradigms to bear on issues in librarianship.

The following is Langenberg's (1989, 13) view of "what a typical scholar might have in the foreseeable future." A workstation might include:

1)   a computer with substantial processing power and ample memory;
2)   a capability to read and store data from a variety of sources, ranging from very high density permanent records, optical disks perhaps, to very high rate data streams from outside;
3)   a versatile interface with its operator, probably primarily visual, to take advantage of the unique capabilities of the human eye-brain system;
4)   a capability to produce output in a variety of forms   including high-resolution, high-speed visualizations for its operator, high-rate electronic data streams for other computers, and symbols and pictures on paper for the anachronistic;
5)   software capable of supporting and amplifying the scholar's skill in dealing with information and communication in many ways, from simple word processing to the manipulation and exploration of complex data sets with the aid of an artificially intelligent electronic partner.

Langenberg (1989, 15) further proposes that the information place of the future "will bear less resemblance to today's library than a modern automobile bears to a nineteenth-century carriage, whether horse-drawn or horseless." He also envisions the functions of the information professional, but insists this person be called an "inforum" that he or she not be a librarian. The three functions of this person evidently sound more familiar to those of us within the Library/Information Science professions than to the author, the distinguished chancellor of the University of Illinois at Chicago. Langenberg states:

> The fundamental functions of an inforum, as I envision it, would include:
>
> 1) providing his or her client scholars with open and convenient access to information and communication resources of all kinds;
> 2) nurturing a community of professional information technologists dedicated to maintaining and improving inforum services to scholars; and
> 3) supporting and maintaining a competitive market in ideas and products related to the generation and use of information.

People and Experience

People and their experience also influence the direction that library education and practice will take. Many faculty now teaching in graduate programs earned their PhDs in the 1960s and 1970s, in the era before the microwave or personal computer, fax machine or satellite transmissions. Many became experts in content areas related to libraries before OPACS and before the emergence of bibliographic instruction as a major role in reference service. They wrote dissertations about bibliographic control without the benefit of OCLC, or described hierarchical organizations with few women as administrators. The world of practice has changed significantly during their careers.

Recent studies predict that the greying of the faculty in academia, including library science, will lead to high changeovers among faculties in the coming years. While retirement may change the actors, it is not necessarily a solution. We must ask whether the current PhD students are viewing the world of information with a new lens in order to conduct research using more applicable methodologies, or developing curricular ideas incorporating an introduction of the new philosophy that will lead to the information literacy ideals. Ideas they are developing as PhD students, they will soon be teaching. Are they yet developing theories, investigating complex phenomena, inventing a heterarchial order, or visualizing holographic images? If not, they too will teach the paradigm within which they studied, the old paradigm, one that is not ready to include information literacy.

Another constant that influences library education is that today's graduate programs are viewed through the rear view mirror of our own master's programs. Students are seldom asked, "What are you learning that I didn't study?" The worst example of this is the librarian who asked a student several years ago, "When are you graduating? I'll be so glad when you stop reading." Alumni frequently scold deans and faculty because students cannot do what they could do when they graduated.

Moving from the first to second generation education means changing ourselves. Harlan Cleveland (1990, 38) reminds us that the main obstacles to change "are in our heads," the "win-lose, we-they scenarios...engraved on people's brains." In *The Age of Unreason*, Charles Handy (1989) suggests that if we are learning, we are changing; if we aren't changing, we aren't learning.

In short, the changes necessary in library school curricula will only occur when a new paradigm emerges that influences practice, teaching, research, attitudes, and values. The people engaged in teaching, research, and practice must encourage rather than discourage the emerging paradigm. Four areas in which change is becoming evident are in the philosophy of library education, the emerging focus on information transfer, a demise of territoriality, and the response to the need for alternative systems to deliver professional education.

Shift in Philosophy

Just as social shifts require rethinking our personal and collective philosophies, so it is necessary to reexamine our philosophy of Library/Information Science education. As the paradigms of the academic disciplines associated with library education and the actions of information professionals are shifting, as technological developments allow alternative patterns, a basic change in the values emphasized in library education is necessary. Change needs to occur among library educators and among the constituency that must support innovation in library education.

The philosophical focus of "people first," as the major framework for Library/Information Science education, is in keeping with shifts in other disciplines. For example, Tom Peters (1987) recommends that people in the workplace must be obsessed with people if organizations are going to survive. While this is not a foreign idea in librarianship, it must become central to the education, research, and practice of this field. The call of bibliographic instruction librarians for more interaction between faculty and librarians has been a healthy influence on the book-centered paradigm. The call now for an expansion of the bibliographic instruction concepts to information literacy and information analysis is certainly an indication of increased response to people's information needs.

In a society of constant change, the graduate school goal must be to impart a philosophy of "people first" to students and to put this into action by creating learning experiences that will require flexibility, problem solving and critical thinking within the framework of client needs.

The earlier expectation of graduate school as a source of specific practical training for a particular workplace is impractical in what Peters (1987) calls an era of customization, niche building, and user responsiveness. The emerging practice of librarianship, certainly the specifics of information literacy drawn out in other chapters of this publication, indicates a need for practitioners who can customize rather than homogenize.

Shift from Biblio-Transfer to Information-Transfer

Bibliographies, bibliographic control, and bibliographic instruction--the root *biblio*, indicates books. It is not suggested that any of these three items are, or have been, invalid, but this author would urge that they should no longer occupy a central place in library education.

If the focus in curricula is broadened to INFORMA-TION (recorded, visual, oral, and graphic) TRANSFER (including creation, diffusion, and utilization), the library profession has a greater chance that the first learned behaviors of graduates will be broad rather than narrow.

For example, the courses such as, "Bibliography of the Social Sciences" should be shifted to "Information Transfer Among the Social Sciences," and that shift must be more than a cosmetic change. Examining the nature of recorded, visual, oral, and graphic information in the social sciences plus the investigation of how these forms of information are created, diffused, and used by people in all and each of the social sciences gives new graduates the knowledge needed to interact with social science faculty in order to customize library services to their research and teaching needs. Of course it is necessary to be familiar with the resources that have been created in the social sciences and the technologies available for disseminating information in the academy and in the practice of each social science. In order to learn how information is transferred within the social sciences, it is necessary for students to examine methods of diagnosing information needs. The experience of actually doing so while in graduate school would certainly enhance a graduate's confidence and perhaps lead to the experience of publishing or co-authoring. Finally, focusing on information transfer in the social sciences prepares a student to be ready to integrate social science information literacy goals into the social science curriculum.

Shift from Type of Library Course to Functions Course

Another of the shifts occurring in Library/Information Science is increased interaction among the previously isolated territories of school, academic, public, and special libraries. The distant learning student is asking for material from the nearest library, not his or her university. The writer who searches databases at his or her workstation at home or work wants access as quickly as possible and seldom thinks about which librarian is appropriate to ask.

Whether at conferences, in conversations, or in the literature, the concepts of information literacy are being expressed by librarians working in a variety of locations. For example, the American Association of School Librarians' publication, *Information Power* (1988), includes similar ideas to those of *Information Literacy* by Brevik and Gee (1989) that was written for academic administrators. Special librarians have long participated in ascertaining the value of documents for researchers.

One alternative to "type of library" courses is to concentrate on the similarities among libraries in order to encourage students to draw ideas from diverse places, literatures, and people, no matter the particular setting in which they work. Furthermore, a curricula that crosses types of libraries prepares today's graduates to fulfill the prediction that they will change jobs and careers often.

An alternative to "turf" courses is "functions" classes as the advanced management courses.   For example, in an Educational Functions course, information literacy can be examined as a concept needed in the schools, the community, and the workplace, as well as the university.   Students can experience the fears of preparing and giving a lecture, designing and delivering a learning exercise, planning and marketing a program.   They can also learn about the structures of systems of higher education, K-12, continuing education, corporate training programs, or adult independent learning centers and examine the role of the library and the librarian in such systems.

Shift Toward Distance Education

Technology not only influences the practice and research of librarianship, it affects the delivery of quality library education programs.   There are fifty-nine accredited library science programs in the United States and Canada, but those programs are located in only thirty-two states, six provinces, Washington, DC, and Puerto Rico.   The demographics of people choosing to enter library science programs make it very difficult for students to pack and move. Residents in geographically disadvantaged areas and the professionals in those states have become increasingly vocal in their demand for alternative delivery systems.

The Library and Information Science Distance Education Consortium (LISDEC), formed in 1990, now includes fourteen accredited Library/Information Science programs that are committed to producing video courses to be shared by the other schools and transmitted over Mind Extension University (soon to be renamed The Education Network), the Jones Intercable Network. It is interesting to note that LISDEC membership includes fewer producing schools than members such as state library agencies, state departments of education, and professional organizations that wish to purchase or lease the courses produced by the schools for purposes of continuing education. (For more information contact the author or Dr. Dan Barron, University of South Carolina, College of Library and Information Science, Columbia, South Carolina 29208).

As more states develop the information highways needed for distribution of two-way interactive courses, the need for faculty to teach beyond the classroom walls will increase. It is quite likely, indeed imperative, that mediated instruction will supplement the weekend intensive courses now available to students in such cities as Sioux City, Iowa, and Denver, Colorado, or the summers-only opportunities available at several universities.

With distance learning opportunities come additional challenges. The interlibrary loan networks, the bibliographic databases and shared catalogs available throughout North America make it increasingly easy for students to identify the resources they wish to examine. The delivery systems are improving in many states, but along with this must come the willingness of librarians to accept local residents as clients of all libraries.

Conclusion

During the Think Tank discussion on the topic of education far beyond the second generation of bibliographic instruction librarians, support for distance learning was very strong. The group supported the development of the consortium (LISDEC) and recommended that professionals throughout the United States actively support such efforts. Without such efforts librarians will not transcend the reality of large segments of the profession who do not have access to professional education, continuing education, or faculty research consulting.

It was also evident that the participants endorsed a new paradigm for library education, one that would be shared profession wide. Participants recommended that the emerging curriculum place greater emphasis on people over resources, and more active incorporation of problem solving practice into course work. It was also recommended that a collegial relationship between students and professionals be stressed, particularly in distance learning environments. It is also important to update the techniques used to evaluate instruction and assess student progress. Finally, it was agreed that leadership and risk-taking must be supported in the context of both library education and the practice of librarianship.

The issues left unresolved included the fear that distance learning efforts would be hampered because turf and territory are so predominant in higher education. The discussion ended with the challenge to think of how librarians could connect information literacy issues to distance learning throughout the curriculum rather than isolating it to only one course.

Author's Note: Allison V. Level attended Think Tank II and contributed to the discussion and thus to the ideas in this paper. She is now employed by the Library of Congress.

References

American Association of School Librarians. 1988. *Information power*. Chicago: American Library Association.

Breivik, Patricia Senn and E. Gordon Gee. 1989. *Information Literacy: Revolution in the library*. New York: American Council on Education and Macmillan.

Cleveland, Harlan. 1990. "The age of spreading knowledge." *The Futurist* (September/October): 33-40.

Handy, Charles. *The age of unreason*. 1990. Boston: Harvard Business School and McGraw-Hill.

Kuhn, Thomas S. *The structure of scientific revolutions*. 2nd ed. 1970. Chicago: University of Chicago Press.

Langenberg, D. N. 1989. "Supporting the global scholar." *Academic Computing*. 3, no. 5 (January) 12-16.

Peters, Tom. 1987. *Thriving on chaos*. New York: Harper & Row.

THE FUTURE OF BIBLIOGRAPHIC INSTRUCTION AND INFORMATION LITERACY FOR THE ACADEMIC LIBRARIAN

William Miller

The concept of "Bibliographic Instruction" appears to be one of the great success stories of modern American academic librarianship. It is difficult now to remember that the Bibliographic Instruction Section (BIS) of the Association of College and Research Libraries (ACRL) was founded little more than a decade ago, and that those who founded it were looked upon by many as wild-eyed radicals. BIS soon became the largest activity section within ACRL, and has remained among the most successful because the membership has worked tirelessly in large numbers to insure that "BI" would prevail.

Bibliographic instruction did in fact prevail, and it has long since been enshrined in job advertisements, in the activities of Reference Departments, and occasionally even in separate departments of its own. As a result, it is now taken for granted that instruction will be a core task for reference librarians. A negativist could now say that bibliographic instruction is "politically correct." In broader terms, during the last decade the concept of an academic library's mission has been expanded to include proactive instructional efforts, so much so that if a library mission statement did not include instruction, the oversight would immediately be pointed out.

Academic Librarians' Role as Teachers

Underlying this success is the assumption that academic librarians have a role to play as teachers. Society as a whole has never fully ascribed this role to librarians, and even within the profession there has been some ambivalence. In the earlier days of "the movement," there was reluctance to teach, which for some was a reluctance to assume or usurp the teaching faculty's prerogative. As related by Olson (1990, 7) there is still a feeling among some public, academic, and special librarians that their clients pay taxes, tuition, or corporate funds to obtain "librarians' expertise, not to be told to take a bibliographic instruction course."

A more convincing argument against teaching is the "Delphic" argument--the notion that teaching people to find information is both counterproductive to librarians' own interests and contrary to human nature. Even the esteemed library educator Herbert S. White (1990, 55) calls for librarians to be intermediaries rather than instructors:

> We try to insist that they learn, for reasons I do not completely understand, because perhaps we should stress instead that they ask librarians. Fewer people now repair their own cars, and fewer people do their own tax returns. Why is it important that more people do their own library searches, as long as the searches are done and done well?

Clearly enough there are circumstances, especially in corporate libraries, in which librarians are paid to provide information only, rather than to teach people how to find it. And perhaps, as Briggs et al. (1985) concur, there is also a case to be made for establishing librarianship as a Delphic mystery, the secrets of which must be protected either in the interests of library users or, more likely, in the interests of librarians themselves.

Most academic librarians would agree, however, that there must also be a stronger case made for circumstances in which it is highly appropriate that librarians teach, and empower students and others to become independent learners and researchers. If any branch of librarianship has a clear responsibility to teach, it certainly must be academic librarianship, in concert with the rest of the academic enterprise. Indeed, the whole concept of faculty status for librarians, for those who believe in that concept as the ACRL division of ALA officially does (1975), hinges on the notion that academic librarians must be more than handmaidens in the teaching enterprise.

Information Literacy-the Second Phase

During the last decade, the bibliographic instruction movement has swept away most objections to teaching, and it has become an established practice in American academic libraries. In the midst of all this success, however, there is also a growing feeling that bibliographic instruction itself is insufficient, as it has traditionally been practiced, to carry the library profession into the electronic age. As Anita Kay Lowry said in "Beyond BI: Information Literacy in the Electronic Age" (1990, 23), instructional efforts must now burst "the usual boundaries of bibliographic instruction to include personal information management, the systems of scholarly communication, and computer-assisted textual research."

The degree to which instructional expectations are changing is well expressed in a recent (1991) position announcement posted on the PACS-L electronic mail list. The advertisement is for an "Information Management Education Librarian" for a medical library, and sets as one goal the improvement of "users' skills in information problem solving, retrieval, and management." The duties of the position include:

> using client-centered approaches to develop, market, teach, and evaluate credit courses, curriculum-integrated classes, and workshops; providing information management software support, including bibliographic formatting software; and assisting with local database production.

As the terminology and content of the advertisement indicate, the excitement that so many librarians felt about bibliographic instruction in academic librarianship ten years ago now seems in the process of being transferred to the concept of information literacy. Information literacy has been discussed and debated by many in the profession, and has been defined in the ALA committee publication, *American Library Association Presidential Committee on Information* (1989, 6) as the ability to "find, evaluate, and use information effectively to solve a particular problem or make a decision." To many, this notion of information literacy is either synonymous with bibliographic instruction or is a natural outgrowth of that concept that does not represent a radical departure--a rose by another name, yet still a rose. Increasingly, however, there is also a strong sense that teaching information literacy is in fact different from bibliographic instruction, which has not historically entailed the ability to navigate through Bitnet and Internet, the ability to tap into distant databases, and the ability to manage one's own data electronically and dynamically.

In truth, a term such as "Information Management" or "Information User Education" would probably be more appropriate than "Information Literacy" within the context of academic librarianship. The word "literacy" carries with it the connotation of illiteracy, and the continuing implication that librarians are dealing with clients on a basic or even on a remedial level. The library profession will not wish to announce to higher education faculties that academic librarians are engaged in a perpetual quest to provide remediation, to them or to their students. Even if such a quest were true at the moment, it would not be true forever, and it is in any case preferable to describe these efforts in more professional terms.

However, information literacy is the new buzz word, the new umbrella term, and there are real advantages at the moment to using it. As Mary Reichel (1990, 46) points out:

> Besides providing a real link to the nonlibrary world, the use of information literacy has the potential to lead to a more uniform approach between academic and public librarians about the intellectual abilities we want citizens to have. Bibliographic instruction does not fit into the context of the public library, but information literacy ties into the literacy campaign for reading skills which is very much a part of public library services. Information literacy is also valuable because it puts the emphasis on the user, not the librarian, as bibliographic or library instruction does.

The terminology is still being debated.

A decade ago, academic librarians were looking forward to the publication of Beaubien, Hogan, and George's book *Learning the Library* (1982). Librarians are now expecting the publication of Hannelore Rader and Trish Ridgeway's forthcoming book entitled *Information Literacy: A How-To-Do-It*

Manual for Librarians (1991). According to the publisher's advertisement:

> This manual fills the need for a practical guide to help librarians and teachers understand, plan, and teach information literacy for students on all levels and in all subject areas. The authors cover the theoretical foundations of information literacy, integrating it into the curriculum, specific methods of teaching information literacy, and how to build partnerships with teaching faculty.

From the sound of things, librarians may never again see a book with the phrase "Bibliographic Instruction" in its title. However, before taking collective leave of bibliographic instruction, as a term if not as an activity, it would be useful to examine its strengths and weaknesses for signs of where academic librarianship can go with this movement in coming years. This will be a bumpy ride rather than a smooth transition. In fact, it will not be easy to translate the success of bibliographic instruction into an easy continuum of instruction for information literacy in the 1990s.

Information Literacy and the New Generation of Users

Bibliographic instruction has concerned itself with instruction in the use of the bibliographic apparatus created by librarians in order to provide access to the universe of printed materials traditionally acquired by libraries. Bibliographic instruction has been successful in part because researchers, and in particular student researchers, have been forced to depend on traditional library materials, housed in traditional library

buildings, and have been forced as well to depend on the
assistance of librarians as their navigators.

In the broader world of information literacy, the library
profession will be on more nebulous ground. The truth is that
librarians have enjoyed the power and the control that have
come with being the center of the information universe, and
librarians have *not* been especially interested in turning users
into independent consumers of information. The universe of
information seekers is now becoming much more varied, and
much less dependent on librarians, bibliographic apparatus, or
even physical libraries. As the Faxon Company (1991, 7)
discovered in a recent study of the information seeking habits
of professionals in academic, research, and business environments:

> a preference for electronic modes of access is
> apparent among younger professionals in general,
> and computer professionals in particular. Work-
> ers in private organizations are more frequent
> users of new technology, and if the cost barriers
> to online access can be overcome, it appears that
> usage among the entire studied population would
> increase dramatically.

Traditional bibliographic instruction will not take
academic librarians far with this newer generation of researchers, and eventually librarians will also be hard-put to satisfy the
core undergraduate population with traditional bibliographic
instruction efforts. As the profession moves into information
literacy, the clients will be freed from the holds librarians have
been imposing through bibliographic control, ownership of
materials, and occupancy of the building.

From Bibliographic Instruction
to Information Literacy

Bibliographic instruction has been successful in large part because it was ideally suited not only to librarians' own interests, but also to the wider interests and structures of academia. It has achieved acceptance during the past decade in large part because it has proven itself very malleable to the norms of academic instruction. Its normal mode of delivery has been the fifty-minute one-shot lecture, which not coincidentally is also the normal mode of delivery for the rest of academia. Theresa B. Mensching's recent survey in *Research Strategies* (1989) indicates that this approach to bibliographic instruction has not changed appreciably during the past decade.

The fifty-minute approach to information is easily organized and conducted, but inherently superficial--rather like a television show in which all subjects, regardless of their complexity, are presented, and all conflicts resolved within a preset time frame. Very often, all that can really be learned in such a session (and all that librarians have really tried to teach in such a session) is that there is a way of discovering information, and that there are librarians who know how to do so and who can be approached for help, when the time comes. Such a method fosters dependency rather than mitigating it. In fairness to librarians, it must be said that this level of effort was often the best that could be achieved under the circumstances, and it must also be said that the educational system itself is still built largely on the passive receipt of information rather than active involvement in the learning process. Is it possible to expect more of librarians than of assistant professors? Superficially practiced bibliographic instruction (and yes, there are other kinds) may not teach much about libraries, and certainly it teaches much less about the management of information, but it has been extremely useful as a way of gaining access to large groups of students through the academic course structure.

Bibliographic instruction's weakness, then, has also been its strength. It has been able to accommodate itself to the prepackaged format, content, and culture of academia that, in this country at least, divides all knowledge into bite-sized credit units that are controlled by other people. Librarians have been there, with prepackaged presentations, to serve a variety of functions including that of baby-sitter when the instructor had a dentist appointment.

Information Literacy
What are the Barriers?

Now, how can the library profession move from bite-sized to byte-sized? So much of what passes for education, even for higher education in this country is little more than the ingestion of predigested pabulum. Yet such a process is antithetical to the very definition of information literacy. It will be quite a challenge for librarianship to move in a concerted fashion beyond the one-shot forays into the bibliographic apparatus of one field. Look, for instance, at the current course at Columbia University for humanities graduate students--an eight-session course (two hours per session) for 1.5 credits--as described by Lowry (1990, 23):

> This course is designed to introduce graduate students in the humanities disciplines to resources in print and electronic formats that are funda-mental to advanced humanities research. Topics covered by the course include: major reference tools, including computerized online and CD-ROM databases; microcomputer databases for

> managing personal notes and bibliographies; scholarly communication and publishing; and machine-readable texts, textual analysis, and critical editing.

Impressive? Yes, but please note also that the course has only enrolled six students per semester, not for lack of interest but for lack of resources. Lowery goes on to say, "Ideally, G4000 would be taken by all Columbia humanities and history graduate students within their first two years of study, but that is not feasible yet" (Lowry, 1990, 25). Certainly this situation is not a new one. Michigan State University was conducting a similar series of intensive faculty and graduate student seminars that focused on new technology ten years ago, and found similarly that the interest was there but that the resources to carry out the program were hard to find and even more difficult to sustain. Quite simply, Reference Departments--and the libraries of which they are a part--are not set up as true teaching departments, and while this was not necessarily a big problem when the major teaching effort was bibliographic instruction, it will be a continuing barrier to meaningful information literacy programs. Large-scale, meaningful information literacy efforts in large academic libraries may be a practical impossibility.

Information literacy may have a brighter future in smaller college situations, where librarians have been able to get beyond the superficiality of one-shot lectures and workbooks, and into something that approximates a thorough-going information literacy program. The science instruction programs at Earlham College, and their current experimentation with making the Dialog databases available free of charge to all on campus, are brought to mind. For librarians at larger institutions, an alternative path to meaningful information literacy instruction may be through amalgamation with computer centers and other units in a larger teaching (and perhaps administrative) structure. Another alternative could involve leadership in, and perhaps management of, a Campus Wide Information System (CWIS), or an information utility such as an affiliate of the National Public Telecomputing Network (e.g., the Cleveland Freenet). In any case, it will clearly be difficult to engage in information literacy where librarians no longer control the means of production, access, or distribution. Librarians must find ways to become involved *outside* the traditional role of being handmaidens to the course structure.

It will not be easy to make this change. Bibliographic instruction is a classic compromise that has succeeded because it met almost everyone's needs. What was revolutionary is now establishment, and entrenched interests will tend to be conservative about changing that which is comfortable, that which has worked in the past. Academic librarians, especially those seeking parity as faculty members, have seized upon bibliographic instruction as an important factor in establishing their legitimacy within the academic enterprise--but of course information literacy has even more potential to establish this legitimacy, though it is more difficult to carry out.

Faculty members may also resist a move towards information literacy. They have found bibliographic instruction to be a useful adjunct to their teaching efforts, and one that has not threatened to displace them in any way. Can they be comfortable with librarians who truly seize the mastery of information and in the process declare the traditional academic course structure as too confining to allow adequate expression to the information literacy process?

Rarely, outside of librarianship, has bibliographic instruction been spoken of as a discipline or a field of knowledge. It is clear that faculty members think of the Master of

Library Science--even when it has become the Master of Library and Information Science--as a technical and not a substantial degree. On a psychosocial level, bibliographic instruction represents, along with reference work, a level of instructional activity that is tolerable to the academic public. These two public service activities have represented the profession's best chance to convince the rest of academia that the library field represents more than a narrow set of technical skills. But clearly they have been insufficient to convey that message so far, and the widespread closing of schools of library and information science is a result. Administrators, perhaps true to the form that they learned while members of the faculty, consider the "science" aspect of library science to be a joke rather than a reality, and the course of study for librarianship inappropriate at research universities attempting to teach concepts and advance the frontiers of human knowledge. The teaching of information literacy probably represents the best hope to move beyond limiting preconceptions about the library field, but it remains to be demonstrated that librarians will take the initiative, or be given the opportunity should they wish to take it, to perform the tasks that will lift the profession above the limitations under which it now labors.

On a broader level, the very ethos of the society in which librarians function will make information literacy more difficult to achieve than bibliographic instruction was to practice. Bibliographic instruction, with its predominantly fifty-minute ease of application, is easy and seductive, and librarians have been seduced by it themselves, too often to their detriment. Society in general favors processes that are quick, painless, and results-oriented rather than process-oriented. Bibliographic instruction fits well into this frame of mind. The goal is immediate, concrete, and rarely more than twenty or thirty minutes away from completion. For librarians, it is an hour in the weekly schedule. For the faculty member, it is a forfeited class period that does not interfere unduly with the major agenda, which all too often is that particular faculty member's attempt to inculcate a plethora of facts that will promptly be forgotten as soon as the final exam is crammed for and taken. For the students, it is a welcome break in the class routine, a momentary diversion that may have some concrete benefit in terms of making the final paper easier to write.

But true information literacy cannot be obtained in fifty minutes. It is an ongoing process, a time-consuming process, and not an end likely to have value in itself. Those who try to teach it in fifty minutes cannot succeed, and their efforts will not be much valued by society. The easy, superficial, triage approach to reference and instruction are soothing in the short run, but cannot bring ultimate success in an era of electronic access to information.

Will Academic Librarians
Take Up the Challenge?

The ultimate question about information literacy, therefore, would appear to be whether or not academic librarians will have the courage to seize upon it and attempt to implement it, not as bibliographic instruction by another name, but rather as a new and more fully realized expression of their mission as teachers. The belief that librarians are teachers, even if it is ultimately, as Pauline Wilson says, an "organizational fiction" (1979), has nevertheless operated as a powerful mythos that has impelled the growth of professionalism in the library field. In fact, the acceptance of bibliographic instruction as described at the beginning of this article is actually a gradual acceptance, at least within the library profession, of the legitimacy of this role for academic librarians.

There does not appear to be much choice about whether or not to embrace this challenge. Without a commitment to teaching, librarians will never succeed in fostering information literacy in any meaningful way, and the esteem in which the profession is held will decline in proportion to the degree to which the more traditional services become irrelevant. As collection building becomes less important, and information access becomes more important, it seems *inevitable* that the notion of the teaching library will become the primary one to which the profession aspires, while the notion of the repository library where the users must learn to fend for themselves will become almost a thing of the past.

With bibliographic instruction, academic librarians had a very abbreviated kind of teaching, which could be presented in short order on a very limited topic by any librarian with a good personality and a modicum of knowledge. With information literacy, however, librarians have a much more detailed, extensive, and technologically oriented kind of teaching that requires effort and organization of a different order of magnitude. As a result academic libraries as a whole will have to be organized differently if they wish to succeed in this endeavor. Resources will have to be concentrated on access, and recruitment and training will need to focus on technology and instructional technique. The difficulties inherent in all of these changes will indeed be formidable.

Conclusion

Regardless of how willing the profession is to move from bibliographic instruction to information literacy, there remains open the question of whether society will grant librarians the right to play this teaching role. It was easy enough to let librarians into the classroom to do bibliographic instruction for fifty minutes, but to allow academic libraries to become major teaching units that generate no tuition income is another matter. This country has no tradition of viewing libraries, even academic libraries, as more than warehouses that offer triage service. So the road ahead will be difficult at best.

Still, there are some comforting aspects about the situation. First, there inevitably will be many librarians who will know how to make sense of the complexity of information access in coming years, and who will also be able to translate this complexity usefully for others. Any untrained person can tap on keys and come up with screens, but only the trained individual can structure a relevant search and interpret the results. As the people who will be doing this work constantly, librarians will be in an excellent position to assist people, especially if librarians bring subject expertise to bear on their technical abilities.

Second, many librarians are in fact gifted teachers, and most librarians are motivated by an intrinsic desire to teach and to help others. The computer center people have always had a lot of information under their control, but they cannot teach, nor do they wish to do so. Their only aim is to be instrumental rather than primary in the educational process. Nor are nonlibrarian faculty members, sad to say, overly interested in teaching their students to be independent consumers of information. Librarians remain the only group of knowledge workers interested in and potentially capable of helping students and others to find information, synthesize it, and interpret it.

Third, people are already accustomed to coming to librarians for help with information needs. It is usually at a point much too late in the process to be optimal. Librarians do not usually have the chance to exercise the full range of their skills, but it is a start. Librarians do occupy the high ground as service professionals whose skills are sought, and this need can be developed.

Fourth, librarians do have a high degree of credibility in society. People may not understand what academic librarians do, and they may not think of librarians as having a discrete discipline, but they do find whatever it is that librarians do credible. They do not think that librarians profit unduly from the misery of others, and they do not think of suing librarians for malpractice, even where they find an individual to be incompetent. This is of some comfort and can be built upon.

And last, librarians are the only profession that has any hope of gaining a comprehensive grasp of all information and knowledge as a whole, rather than just one narrow part of it, and being able to translate any given part of it to a broad range of people. As the profession moves from the age of bibliographic instruction to the age of information literacy, therefore, it appears that librarians *can* in fact succeed, but only if librarians are true to the best that is within their profession. If the library profession falls back on partial and superficial solutions, librarians individually will fall away from the mainstream and be swept away. Let all librarians hope that collectively the profession can rise to the challenge, and embrace information literacy as the last but also the best hope not just for survival, but also for growth and change.

References

American Library Association Presidential Committee on Information Literacy. 1989. Chicago: American Library Association.

Association of College and Research Libraries. 1975. *Faculty status for academic librarians: A history and policy statements*. Chicago: American Library Association.

Beaubien, Anne K., Sharon A. Hogan, and Mary W. George. 1982. *Learning the library: Concepts and methods for effective bibliographic instruction*. New York: Bowker.

Biggs, Mary, et al. 1985. "Replacing the fast food drop in with gourmet information service: A symposium," *Journal of Academic Librarianship* 11 (May): 68-78.

The Faxon Company. 1991. "Who are your clients?" The *Faxon Report* 2 (Summer): 1, 7.

Lowry, Anita Kay. 1990. "Beyond BI: Information literacy in the electronic age," *Research Strategies* 8 (Winter): 22-27.

Mensching, Theresa. 1989. "Trends in bibliographic instruction in the 1980s: A comparison of data from two surveys," *Research Strategies* 7 (Winter): 4-13.

Olson, Renee. 1990. "Give expertise, not a course," *Library Journal* 115 (15 May): 7.

Rader, Hannelore B. and Trish Ridgeway. 1991. *Information literacy: A how-to-do-it manual for librarians*. New York: Neal-Schuman, forthcoming.

Reichel, Mary. 1990. "Library Literacy", RQ 30 (Fall, 1990): 1, 46.

University of North Carolina Health Sciences Library. "Position announcement: Information management education librarian." Posting on PACS-L. 22 June, 1991.

White, Herbert. 1990. "Libraries and librarians in the next millenium," *Library Journal* 115 (15 May): 55.

Wilson, Pauline C. 1979. "Librarians as teacher: The study of an organization fiction," *Library Quarterly* 49 (April): 146-62.

EDUCATIONAL ROLES OF ACADEMIC LIBRARIES: STATE OF THE ART and an AGENDA FOR THE FUTURE

Randall Hensley
Beth Sandore

Appendix: Summary Document

The Summary Document of the BIS Think Tank II was the first tangible outcome of this two day effort to determine the changing educational roles of academic libraries. Written by Randall Hensley, University of Washington and Beth Sandore, University of Illinois, Urbana-Champaign, the document was used as an initial report to the ACRL, Bibliographic Instruction Section Advisory Council. Subsequent early reports about the Think Tank that appeared in *C&RL News* were also based upon this document.

Hensley and Sandore acted as recorders and summarizers throughout the Think Tank presentations and discussions. It was they who saw an emerging overall structure for the comments and desired results of the discussions. The concept of "action plan" became a unifying structure for the myriad of statements, data, conjecture, and questions generated by the day and a half deliberations. Therefore the summary of each of the four major topics are divided into: major points, suggested objectives, and questions that would influence resolutions or outcomes.

It was hoped that this summary document, in and of itself, could facilitate discussion and initial action on the part of concerned librarians around the country. The then prevalent phrase, "a thousand points of light", while being fuel for a lot of good natured joking, became a general strategy for the Think Tank in terms of overriding outcome. The desire was to diversify responses to the issues the Think Tank identified; to create a response structure that enabled individuals and institutions to understand the trends seen by the Think Tank; and to develop outcomes and considerations that were appended here when the publication was sent to individuals who heard or read about the Think Tank and wanted to know what had happened.

Group 1: Information Literacy

Presenters: Bill Coons, Cornell University
               Hannelore Rader, Cleveland State University

Major Points:

    1)   Managing a response to information literacy

       Implementing from the top and the bottom
       Ceasing or altering present activities and services
       Personnel and personality issues
       Organizational support for change agents

    2)   Changing labels, i.e. examining definitions of "bibliographic instruction," "user education," and "information literacy"

    3)   Scope of response to information literacy

       An ALA-wide concern
       Linkages to: societal issues
       Higher education issues
       Concerns of other types of libraries
       Public schools
       Individual institutional issues

    4)   Identifying tangible returns

       Clarify concepts and implications prior to action

    5)   Establish relationship between information literacy and economic development

Identify libraries as economic resources

Suggested Objectives:

1) An ALA resolution regarding information literacy

2) Continuing education programs

3) Information/presentation packets

4) Librarians become increasingly assertive and political

5) Develop an information literacy response unit within an organization that will eventually diffuse throughout the organization

6) Establish demonstration sites for initial information literacy related responses and programs

7) Establish evaluation criteria for information literacy related responses and programs

8) Assess current activities and services for cuts which will create time and funding to implement information literacy related responses and programs

9) BIS sponsors conference programs

10) The profession establishes practical action agenda

11) The profession establishes practical outcomes

12) Change the name of BIS and other labels where "bibliographic" is used

13) Identify change agents, e.g. good teachers, administrators, practitioners

Questions:

1) How do we configure organizationally dynamic personnel for taking action related to information literacy?

2) How do we groom administrators for taking action?

3) What are the possible tangible outcomes?

4) Where are libraries culpable for the current state of affairs?

5) How will information literacy concerns impact the historical steadiness of information control?

6) What kinds of changes will be brought about intra-organizationally as different

units and activities meet the challenge of
information literacy?

Group 2: Curriculum Reform

Presenters: Maureen Pastine, Southern Methodist University
               Linda Wilson, Virginia Polytechnic University

Major Points:

1) The curriculum reform movement is problematical.

2) Research skills are increasingly important to students.

3) Student demands upon libraries and their use of them is increasing while their patience for training is decreasing.

4) The image problems of librarians must be enhanced.

5) Librarians need to let go of some traditional services even when they are good.

6) Effort needs to be expended to educate fellow professionals.

7) There is a need to resolve issues surrounding systems instruction vs. concept based instruction.

8) It is important to avoid responding to information literacy issues for the sake of

librarian status--make sure the issues and
the responses are based on user realities.

Suggested Objectives:

1) Create action plans

2) Connect to speakers bureaus

3) Create grant proposals for information
literacy responses

4) Survey employers to establish information literacy response criteria

5) Teach faculty to teach information literacy skills

6) Teach staff to teach including peer group
instruction

Questions:

1) What is the success we want?

2) How do we do instructional design for
transference of information literacy
skills?

3) How has bibliographic instruction teaching changed?

4) Will we be designing new evaluation
   methods?

Group 3: Changing Users: Bibliographic Instruction for Whom?

Presenters: Betsy Wilson, University of Illinois, Champaign-
              Urbana
              Jim Shedlock, Northwestern University

Major Points:

1) Users can be defined in a number of
    ways.Most of us view "everyone" as a
    potential user.

2) Demographics used in defining user
    groups:

    Gender
    Minorities
    Age
    Socio-economic status
    Country of origin
    Societal changes

3) User preparation for library use varies,
    for following reasons:

    Wide disparity in sophistication levels
    Changing learning styles
    Changing user expectations

4) Computers create the belief that time
    can be infinitely compressed.

5) The future promises further moves to-
    ward a pluralistic society and a global
    economy in the United States. This
    future will emphasize the changing na-
    ture of user needs with respect to librar-
    ies.

6) Important to define the relationship
    between computer literacy and informa-
    tion literacy

7) Caveat: technology, the great equalizer,
    has the potential of becoming a great
    unequalizer, e.g. gender gap in computer
    use, haves and have-nots.

8) Faculty are better at teaching skills,
    weaker at teaching concepts, which are
    the basis of most critical inquiry.

9) Reward structure is needed for successful
    work with users in libraries.

10) The relationship between libraries and
    computer centers (especially in the area
    of user services) is still tenuous.

11) Response to change is largely dependent
    on individual personality.

<u>Suggested Objectives:</u>

1) Identify change agents and target students who will be administrators.

2) The "thousand points of light" approach: allow for a diversified response to a common goal for instruction, so that institutions across the country can approach goals in a manner best fit for their environments.

3) Set up a directed reward structure with BIS, ALA, which rewards goals set by the section and organization.

<u>Questions:</u>

1) Are users really everyone? Can we work to create situations where a population of users are related to a particular issue, and study our users more effectively?

2) For what are we planning change? For whom--ourselves, users?

3) Who supplies users' services--computer centers or libraries?

Group 4: Education for the Second Generation of BI Librarians

Presenters: Martha Hale, Emporia State University
               Allison Level, Emporia State University
               Elizabeth Frick, Dalhousie University

Major Points:

1) A new paradigm for library education is
    needed.

2) The concept of a paradigm was explored-
    - paradigm being the lens through which
    one views a particular situation or issue.

3) Change and common characteristics in
    education and the library profession:

    "Small is beautiful"
    Organizations are complex, making it
    difficult to achieve small is beautiful
    Need to look at non-linear, as well as
    linear, learning styles, and develop ways
    to teach both
    Objectivity in research difficult to main-
    tain--perspective research is O.K.
    Shift away from education as a place--to
    education as a process
    Interference between old and new educa-
    tional paradigms occurring

4) Obstacles to effecting change:

First-learned behavior--reinforce old
paradigm
Need for consistency

5) Graduate school objective: to impart a
philosophy and ideals to students vs.
early objective of practical training for
the workplace.

6) Need to move from the difficult concept
of "bibliographic" to the concept of information transfer.

7) Instill a "people first" philosophy in students.

8) Concentrate on understanding the environment, and assessing how information
transfer relates to a particular environ-
ment--public, academic, school.

9) Distance education--in person or via
satellite.

10) Issue of territoriality in library education-
-turf.

Suggested Objectives:

1) Promote a "curriculum in the sky" attitude toward library education.

2) Develop a new paradigm for library education to share profession-wide.

3) Place greater emphasis on process over resources.

4) Pursue more active incorporation of practicum into coursework.

5) Develop updated evaluation techniques for instruction.

6) Create a collegial relationahip with students through the distance education program.

7) Pursue the development of an education video consortium in library education.

8) Actively support leadership and risk-taking in the profession.

Questions:

1) What about the issue of turf in library education?

2) How do we transcend the concept of geographically-located library schools?

3) Distance learning is taking place across the curriculum. How do we connect information literacy issues to distance

learning throughout the curriculum (especially in cases where media is being used)?

ABOUT THE CONTRIBUTORS

Betsy Baker is currently Head of Northwestern University's Reference Library. Previously, she served as Northwestern's Bibliographic Instruction Services Librarian and Coordinator for the CLR funded "Educating the Online Catalog User" project. In 1986 she was elected chair of Association of College and Research Libraries' Bibliographic Instruction Section. She has published extensively in the areas of user education and information retrieval and has presented numerous workshops and lectures on a national and international level on these topics. She remains active nationally in promoting user education activity in libraries of all types.

Bill Coons is currently Head of Reference at Cornell University's Stouffer Hotels Library. Previously, he held positions at Utah State University and Cornell University's Albert R. Mann Library. From July 1989-June 1990 he was the Principal Investigator for the ALA's Carroll Preston Baber Research Grant, and from 1988-1990 he was the Principal Investigator for an Apple Computer Hypercard interface design project (MacPAC). Mr. Coons has co-edited a book on public access CD-Roms, authored a column for *Laserdisk Professional*, written a score of papers on computers, software, and instruction, and has presented many lectures on various topics at regional and national professional meetings.

Elizabeth Frick is currently Associate Professor at Dalhousie's School of Library and Information Studies at Halifax. She spent fifteen years as a librarian at Cornell University, Earlham

College, and the University of Colorado--Colorado Springs in various reference and user service capacities. Professor Frick's current research and publishing is in the areas of bibliographic instruction, public services, and evaluation of service.

Martha Hale is currently Dean of the School of Library and Information Management of Emporia State University. She has been a Peace Corps volunteer, administrative analyst, full-time mother, and community analysis consultant for librarians. She is a past chair of ALA's Library Research Roundtable, and is currently a member of ALA's committee on Outreach Library services, and chair of LISDEC, a national consortium of library schools committed to distance learning. Dean Hale's research areas are community analysis, needs assessment, and information transfer among managers.

Randall Hensley is currently User Education Librarian of the University of Washington Libraries and Acting Head of that university's Odegaard Undergraduate Library. He has taught a course on library user education at the UW Graduate School of Library and Information Science for eight years and is a frequent conference speaker and workshop presenter on such topics as learning styles, training implications of user behavior and online systems, and evaluating sources instruction.

Donald Kenney is currently Assistant to the University Librarian at Virginia Tech's University Libraries. Prior to this position, he served as the Head of the Reference Department at Virginia Tech. He's active in ACRL's BIS where he has served on numerous committees. Mr. Kenney has written and published articles on bibliographic instruction in various journals in librarianship. He co-authored the chapter on research writing in *The Confident Writer*, published by W. W.

Norton. In addition, he has published articles on young adult literature in the *English Journal*, *The ALAN Review*, and the *Journal of Reading*.

Mary Ellen Litzinger is currently Instructional Specialist and Head, Library Studies Program at Penn State University Libraries. She is nationally active in user education organizations and currently chairs the Association of College and Research Libraries's Bibliographic Instruction Section. Her research interests include the development of basic information skills programs, and the use of CAI programs in library user education. Ms. Litzinger is a doctoral candidate in Instructional Systems at Penn State University.

William Miller is currently Director of Libraries and Learning Resources at Florida Atlantic University in Boca Raton, Florida. He served as Chair of Association of College and Research Libraries' Bibliographic Instruction Section from 1984-85 after having been active in the Section for a number of years. Other ACRL appointments have included service as Chair of the *Choice* magazine Editorial Board and membership on the Planning Committee. He is a prolific writer and has numerous articles and book chapters in the literature.

Maureen Pastine is Director of Central University Libraries at Southern Methodist University in Dallas, Texas. She has taught graduate library school courses at the University of Illinois at Urbana-Champaign, San Jose State University, the University of Washington, and Emporia State University. She has published in the areas of library administration, library user education, reference services, and women's studies.

Hannelore Rader is currently Director of the Cleveland State University Library. Previously, she served as Director of the Library Learning Center at the University of Wisconsin-Parkside. Other career experiences include serving as Humanities Librarian, Orientation Librarian and Head of the Education Psychology Division of the Library at Eastern Michigan University. She has been active in the American Library Association and served as president of the Association of College and Research Libraries, chair of numerous committees, and on the Council of ALA. Ms. Rader has spoken on and published articles regarding user instruction and library organization and management.

Beth Sandore is currently Assistant Automated Services Librarian at the University of Illinois Library at Urbana-Champaign. Previously, she held the position of Instruction Librarian at Illinois Institute of Technology and served as Research Associate for Northwestern University's CLR funded "Educating the Online Catalog User" project. Her research and publications focus on developing cognitive models for understanding and teaching information retrieval for online systems.

James Shedlock is currently the Director of Northwestern University's Galter Health Sciences Library. Previously, he held the position of Head of Public Services in the library. He came to Northwestern from the Health Sciences Library at the University of North Carolina at Chapel Hill where he had been the Assistant Head of the Information Services Department and Coordinator of Online Search Services. Mr. Shedlock has also held positions at the Shiffman Medical Library, Wayne State University in Detroit, and at St. Joseph Mercy Hospital Library in Pontiac, Michigan. He has served in a number of positions within the Medical Library Association. Mr. Shedlock has also served and chaired a number of MLA committees and has participated in MLA's Section Council.

Linda Wilson is currently the Coordinator of Reference Services and Education Bibliographer at the University Libraries, Virginia Polytechnic Institute and State University. Her previous experience includes the design and implementation of a user education project linked to the VTLS online catalog as well as the coordination of a comprehensive bibliographic instruction program. Ms. Wilson is presently pursuing another interest as co-editor of the ALA publication, *The Journal of Youth Services in Libraries.*

Lizabeth A. Wilson is currently the Head of the Undergraduate Library, Assistant Director of Libraries for Undergraduate and Instructional Services, and Associate Professor at the University of Illinois at Urbana-Champaign. She has been involved in bibliographic instruction at both the undergraduate and graduate level for over ten years. Her expertise and accomplishment is reflected in the receipt of two undergraduate instructional awards, an Amoco Foundation Award for Improvement in Undergraduate Education, and an excellence in graduate teaching award. She is the current past-chair of the Association of College and Research Libraries Bibliographic Instruction Section. Ms. Wilson has spoken and written widely on education for bibliographic instruction, large-scale instruction programs, and the impact of information technology on user education.